TESTIMONIALS

"As folks across Georgia are still enduring a difficult economic downturn, it's inspiring to see citizens joining hands to aid in rebuilding the careers of their neighbors. This effort demonstrates how members of a community can lean upon each other to bring about positive solutions and a better future. Georgia communities have been exemplary in the work they have done to put folks back to work through education, the promotion of job search skills, coaching, and emotional support. This book is a valuable tool for faith-based community leaders who wish to help their neighbors during a time of hardship."

Tom Price
Congressman, Georgia 6th District
US House Committee on Labor and Education

"Georgia and the nation have suffered the most severe economic downturn since the Great Depression. The increase in state and national unemployment rates and the collapse of banking, housing and construction industries have caused economic havoc. In countering the storm, countless citizens have joined hands to assist our unemployed, underemployed and discouraged workers. Many have joined hands to assist Job Seekers in rebuilding their careers and their lives. Together, we can all reach out to each other and create the economic destinies we seek. In particular, I am proud of the efforts made by faith-based leaders who provide Job Seekers with education, training, coaching and emotional support. *Loving Your Neighbor: a Faith Community's Response to the Unemployment Crisis* is an excellent model for faith based leaders helping others during a time of crisis. This book is a must read and sound tool for community leaders alike."

Michael Thurmond
Georgia Commissioner of Labor

"As CEO of the North Fulton County Chamber of Commerce I have seen the changes in our community as a result of unemployment. Unemployment brings with it a feeling of defeat. North Fulton County is a thriving, robust community of entrepreneurial businesses, upscale homes with top performing and committed educators in our schools. We are all about bringing the best businesses, best people and best forms of transportation to our thriving community. Getting folks back to work is the key to our community's success. The career programs for Job Seekers that have sprung up in our local churches and synagogues have provided excellent ways for employed neighbors to reach out to the unemployed while lending a helping ear. This is not a time to go at it alone! This book proves that a community can reach across the roads and highways to bring about excellence and caring among neighbors."

Brandon L. Beach
President and CEO
Greater North Fulton Chamber of Commerce

In the Book of Acts 1:8 Jesus says…"You will be my witnesses in Jerusalem, and in all Judea and Samaria, and to the ends of the earth." Right now our "Jerusalem," our home town is hurting, and what better way to be His witnesses and to "love our neighbor" than through helping those struggling through the current economic crisis. This book is an inspiration to both those that want to help and to those who need encouragement in their job search.

William N. Goff, Jr. CLU, ChFC

Retired Consultant, Towers Perrin
Former Chairman of the Board, The Mission Society
Professor of Business, LCC International University, Klaipeda, Lithuania

Testimonials

"A community has come together to give of their time and talent to enrich the lives of those who are in transition. We walk away feeling more blessed when we can see that our words and our actions have made someone's day brighter, made them feel more confident and confirmed to them that they are not alone in this journey."

Kathy Earle
Principal, Executive Strategies, Inc.

"When the going gets tough, it is wonderful to know that we have the ability to come together as industry leaders and believers to meet the needs of our communities. Many believe that a line must be drawn in the sand between our work life and our faith life. This book provides an example of how needs can be met when industry leaders walk the talk they believe and give of their time and talent to those in need. Jobs are not just found, lives are changed."

Michelle Lee
President and CEO, DDS Staffing Resources, Inc.
Past President, Georgia Association of Personnel Services

"You do not need to search the globe to find meaningful mission work. Neighbors in our communities are unemployed and hurting. Many feel broken and demoralized. Breadwinners feel they have failed at their life's mission, marriages are strained, and families are stressed.

Many of us are uniquely qualified to help. Being part of a career focused outreach is a meaningful way to do His work in our community. When people are gainfully employed, the fabric of our families, our communities, and our nation is stronger."

Greg Losh
Human Resource Executive
Ministry Leader, Northbrook UMC

"Atlanta Business Bank is proud to say that we were an early supporter of this most valuable resource to the community. When the church needed donations to expand this ministry beyond its previous scope adding a dinner and a supportive ear to Job Seekers, we were fortunate to be able to jump in. This is a true example of private enterprise and the faith based community working hand in hand together to help our neighbors in crisis. This is an inspiring read for all pastors and church leaders who wish to join in this endeavor."

Ed Cooney
President, Atlanta Business Bank

"The aspect that draws me to volunteer efforts is the satisfaction of giving to some other person/persons the gifts that God has given me. The greater good for the greater number makes a lasting impact in any work worth doing. God has provided the door and the weight on my heart to do his will. In the work of assisting our brothers and sisters in finding gainful employment there can be no better example of all these aspects coming together"

Conrad Taylor
Chairman, National Association of Personnel Services

"For over 25 years I have tried helping those finding themselves out of work. As I assist faith based organizations in that endeavor, and ask the Job Seeker to have faith, ask our Lord and Savor to guide us all in their next steps...it always pleases me to see those who have never had faith or fallen away see the warmth and comfort of trusting in our Lord. What a tremendous feeling it is to help 45-60 individuals each year find a job on a suggestion or guidance that I always feel my Heavenly Father allowed me to say or do to guide those successes."

Jim Cichanski
President & CEO
Flex HR, Inc.

Loving Your Neighbor

A Faith Community's Response to the Unemployment Crisis

By

Katherine Simons

Foreword by: Rusty Gordon
First Printing 2010

All scripture quotations, unless otherwise indicated, are taken from the New International Version.

ISBN: 978-0-578-05988-4

Cover Design: Grace Design, Atlanta, Georgia
Apex Book Manufacturing, Alpharetta, Georgia

DISCLAIMER
Any statements of positions or opinions by persons featured in this book (other than Katherine Simons) do not necessarily express the positions or opinions of Katherine Simons or of Roswell United Methodist Church, nor are the statements of positions or opinions of Katherine Simons necessarily the positions or opinions of Roswell United Methodist Church.

DEDICATION

This book is gratefully dedicated to every person who has faithfully supported our ministry over the years and to all the Job Seekers they continue to serve.

TABLE OF CONTENTS

FOREWORD

By Rusty Gordon

Sometimes you will hear an athlete speak about the "Sweet Spot." This is a term used to describe themselves or their team at their very best, as in "I hit it in the sweet spot" or "we were in our sweet spot in that game."

Without question we have learned that the Job Networking Ministry is the *sweet spot* for our church and I suspect it very well may be for yours as well. Before I explain let me introduce myself.

My name is Rusty Gordon and I have been a member of the Roswell United Methodist Church for over 25 years. I have participated in all phases of our church with a special focus as a youth leader for 20 years and a mission leader for nearly as long. The last three years I have also served as Lay Leader of our church and it is from that perspective that I share views on the Job Networking Ministry. My perspective is influenced by the time I have spent in active workplace ministry with High Tech Ministries in Atlanta and with Workplace Ministries which is a nationwide program.

For me the sweet spot is achieved because Job Networking overcomes three great challenges we face in our pursuit to be true to the actual definition of the church which is "Ecclesia" i.e. *Believers linked together in our Lord's will through the Holy Spirit.*

The first challenge we have overcome is that of complacency: we expect the pastor or paid staff and maybe a couple of obsessive volunteers to take our donations and use them effectively to please

God. I call that dirty money but no dirty hands. The very key to our Job Networking Ministry has been the building up of our own disciples while inviting, growing and serving the community in which God has placed us.

This ministry is run entirely by lay "directors". They are all volunteers from both our church and our community who serve side by side with those who are in career transition. On any given meeting over 100 volunteers from a pool of nearly twice that will fill over a dozen different jobs including faith speaker, professional speaker, Table Host, greeter/host, resume reviewer, server (dinner) and many others. As such, this ministry has become our premiere venue for developing passionate disciples for Christ.

In public and private settings, sometimes with hundreds and sometimes one-to-one, our laity works in real community by:

- Sharing their personal faith stories and challenges;
- Offering the good news to those that are hurting;
- Praying intercessory prayers together with guests;
- Inviting new people to share our church home or services;
- Providing critical connections for guests job search;
- Providing professional advice or actual training.

Our ministers' job is to support our lay directors and volunteers and reaffirm that guests are welcome.

In other words, this is where our members move from being churched to being the church. Their spiritual skills and passions are both developed and realized in the repetition of serving others spiritually, physically and emotionally. God continues to present volunteers and our lay directors continue to challenge them to use the ministry to grow. The result is we do not have tired volunteers, but tireless volunteers, serving with purpose.

A second challenge that creeps into our church and other churches is evangelizing without serving or "not walking the talk" as it is sometimes called. Our Job Networking Ministry directly addresses this challenge. The base principle we follow is that there are people with real needs that effect entire families; right here in our very own community and God will send them to our door if we will serve them as He would if He were here.

Therefore our outlandish principle is that we actively recruit "career needy" people. We welcome them when they arrive. We affirm that they are special and we feel privileged to serve them. When they leave, they will have received pragmatic professional and spiritual support for free that is at least as good if not better than any fee based services in our area. Consistently, people share that they are absolutely amazed with the quality of the program and the enthusiasm with which the program opportunities are offered and stunningly for free. Our leaders and our volunteers call that "experiencing the Gospel."

However, the opposite challenge is also one that many churches, especially Methodist churches often face. That challenge is serving without evangelizing or, in other words, "not talking the walk." Francis of Assisi is credited with saying "Preach the gospel and use words when necessary." That is a good direction for our ministry, but we have found that there is a proper time for using words. In fact, we encourage our guests to discuss the gospel and its practical application in our lives. We have lived our faith in service, but we have failed to share our faith in a way that others might learn from our experiences. Our volunteers have discovered that their experiences are useful and motivating to others, that they have a sufficient spiritual base and gift to facilitate another person's discovery of God and His will, that God will bless their side by side intercessory prayers, and that others may even learn how and why to pray. Some have even realized that they can and should share their knowledge and experiences from the podium, and in the process our church has discovered spiritual resources that none of us knew existed in our pews.

So how do you summarize our long journey of service that has suddenly reached its sweet spot. We integrated our *walk* with our *talk* and quit passing off what we are supposed to do to our *professional* staff?

We are a work in progress, of course. But the fruits of the labor have been many already:

- The community of needy at our door step have been served spiritually, emotionally and professionally;
- God sends individuals to us who are seeking more than a job and some who are just lost. We offer a place of comfort and a relationship to those who might be willing to take a step;
- As a body and as individuals we are much better prepared to be useful to our Lord in the future regardless of how He wants the gospel shared;
- As a church we have a model of serving God with a clear purpose;
- We have a constant reminder of the power of prayer, scripture and service.

And all of us continue to learn that God is always at work and our work, whatever it is, is more fulfilling when we work with Him.

And what are we left with? …An energized church and stories. Oh my goodness…stories you must hear. These are stories of amazing events in the lives of our guests, our volunteers and in the lives of the church and our community.

The story of Jesus retold in people's lives.

The lay leader has become a lay observer and it is a sight to behold.

ACKNOWLEDGEMENTS

This book would not have been possible without the help of my loving husband, Craig, whose wise counsel and commitment to excellence propels me forward and to Tim Morrison of Write Choice Services who helped plan, edit, organize the manuscript and spent endless hours holding my hand. I also want to thank the writers for putting their thoughts and feelings on paper, Bruce Kromer for his photography, my dad, Richard (Dick) Fritz a tireless greeter, Dr. Mike Long for his trust and blessing to move ahead, Julie Scott's wonderful kitchen staff, and the original Dream Team for stepping out to expand the ministry. Our sincere appreciation to Bill Goff for naming our book and for endless hours of editing along with my sister, Linda Feierabend, Roger Davis, Mark Lloydbottom and Tom Knight. Special thanks to Mary Schaefer who continues to work through the details of our Job Networking expansion, Rusty Gordon who gives spiritual and practical guidance, John Harper for his prayers and encouragement, and especially to Jay Litton for his continued vision and leadership.

INTRODUCTION

Writing a book is an evolving process. My purpose in writing this book is to provide a "cookbook" for pastors and church leaders, complete with a "menu" of choices designed for starting or expanding a ministry that is focused on helping our unemployed neighbors. I was amazingly surprised, when 35 of the volunteers in our ministry submitted their stories about "why and how" they give their time and talents to Job Seekers.

Inside these pages, you will find a complete description of the elements of a Job Seeker ministry. The pieces can be cut and pasted to form any size church or organization. In the chapter on "New Job Networking Ministries" you will read about how to start tomorrow. You will experience how much fun and reward we receive by partnering with our community to help people in crisis. You will also see that starting and sustaining a program such as this is truly not difficult, when people come together with passion and with a willingness to share from their gifts. Hopefully, you will not miss how a program like this can bring strength and vitality to your congregation, while expanding your reach in your town.

But here's the surprise! I can't wait until you read the stories from the volunteers! These stories are inspiring and often truly captivating. These are real people who were asked to serve (just once) and then willingly continued to come back, time after time. So many discovered that the time they offered was clearly making a difference in someone else's life. Jesus gave us the parable of the Good Samaritan, ending with the instructions to, "go and do likewise." These volunteers know they are being called upon to be that good neighbor. They have heard (and are enjoying) the command, "GO!"

As you read these caring and dynamic stories, you will see that our ministry focus on the unemployed could easily have some other ministry focus and achieved the same results. The same principles that we used to focus on an important need and to harness the gifts of so many volunteers, can work in other volunteer programs, just as effectively. What is critical is that you begin with a small group of passionate individuals who unite around a common purpose to "love their neighbor" and that you continue to give others an opportunity to serve with their unique gifts.

Read, enjoy, laugh (for sure), and perhaps even cry, a bit, but have fun pulling from "this" program recipe, and adding a little of "that", to design your own special mix of ministry which is just right for your congregation.

Blessings!
Katherine

PREFACE

Why we do it!

One night I stood in the back of the room while a speaker was teaching Job Seekers advanced, up-to-date networking skills used by top professionals. I noticed one of our volunteers who had left the resume review team area and was standing by himself. "Greg, are you OK?" Greg hesitated, then, with a painful expression he said "It's been a tough day. It started with a friend I met for breakfast. He's been out of work for four months and has nothing on the horizon. He told me a litany of painful circumstances related to both+ being out of work and to the job search itself. It was difficult to listen to him." But then his friend asked him if he knew the worst part of being out of work. Greg told me that there was a long pause and wet eyes as the man told Greg "My wife doesn't respect me anymore."

How wide and deep is the reach of the many complex tentacles surrounding being out of work! There is a heavy feeling of hopelessness and defeat. Imagination and creativity are lost.

Twenty years ago, a professional recruiter started helping people in career transition at our church. He coached them to prepare for their interviews and gave guidance on ways to prepare a resume. He would help one person or twenty, whoever showed up. He answered their questions and provided counsel. Over time others joined in to help. One evening in 1999, Jay Litton (seeking to offer help) walked in the door looking for the Church's job ministry and found one person seeking help. Jay took this on as a challenge and began developing a professional program with speakers who could teach skills. Jay tried a variety of program formats such as discussion in small groups and sharing leads. He searched for a format that would truly speak to the Job Seekers. He settled on a twice a month schedule (the second and fourth Monday evenings). In the first year of his guidance, the program began drawing 45-50 Job Seekers at each session. Today, an RUMC Job Networking Ministry has from 250-350 Job Seekers in attendance. In addition, there are more than 100 volunteers, on any given night, who help make the program happen.

In the following pages you will learn the simple yet powerful ways you can set up a program that will truly help Job Seekers.

With responsibilities shared among volunteers and nominal funding, you can provide a stellar program.

Moreover you and your volunteers can experience a great deal of fun and satisfaction!

This book presents step by step, the simple yet complete functioning of a growing and vital Job Networking Ministry. We will tell you the real stories of the volunteers, often Job Seekers themselves, and how this ministry changed their lives forever.

CHAPTER 1

"Love the Lord your God, with all your heart and all your soul, and with all your strength." Deuteronomy 6:5

".....love your neighbor as yourself."
Leviticus 19:18

New Job Networking Ministries

One of the most enjoyable aspects of having a successful program is seeing it multiplied in other churches. You will read true stories from community volunteers who became involved at our church and then went back to their churches and started or expanded their home church ministries. Often, leaders and pastors come from other churches to see how our programs can be modified to fit their needs. June 9, 2008, we offered our first dinner program. Within three months of that first dinner, the numbers of Job Seekers in attendance doubled. The North Georgia United Methodist Church Advocacy Committee noticed our growth. The importance of offering an event similar to RUMC Job Networking throughout the Methodist connection of churches was recognized within the committee. Throughout the history of the ministry, we have worked closely with other faith communities who sought to begin their own Job Seeker programs. A year ago, representatives of our ministry spoke to the appropriate judicatory committee in our region and we received the designation of "teaching church." That means that we are recognized and encouraged to teach other congregations, within our denomination and beyond, the steps to creating a Job Seeker ministry. We have always wanted to share our experience with others. Our intention is that this book will help faith communities beyond our region to establish vital programs.

Each element of our program was born one step at a time.

For those congregations interested in starting their own program or ministry, we offer time to their church leaders and pastors to meet with some of our program leaders three hours before our meeting begins.

We engage in lively discussions as we each share experiences in working with Job Seekers. We listen as we ask the leaders and ministers about their hopes and intentions in starting a program. Most of the people who come are completely overwhelmed when they learn of the scope of our program, so we address that concern immediately. It is so important for others to understand that our growth has been organic and natural. Each element of our program was born one step at a time. The various elements evolved as the need for new ministries surfaced and as volunteers stepped up to help. Each of these new offerings came as a result of volunteers offering to help. People love to be part of a successful program.

Build off the strength and gifts of the leaders and volunteers.

During these one-to-one meetings, we walk through the purpose of the ministry, how we started, how we get and keep volunteers, how and why we offer workshops, how we develop our speaker list, why we think it is important to have a speaker, why we added a dinner, what are the costs, database management, how we bring in Job Seekers, and other program ideas. Our purpose is to give an overview and perspective of the ministry.

After we talk from 3:00 to 4:30 p.m., our leader guests become part of the set up of the program, join the Job Seekers at a dinner table, meet our volunteers, listen to an inspiring and thought provoking talk and participate in a table discussion led by a volunteer facilitator. Following the dinner program ending at 7:00 p.m., they visit the workshops being held, or see our prayer partners in the chapel as they pray with Job Seekers who go to the chapel seeking prayer. Some choose to sit at an industry specific networking table or to learn how Industry Guides works.

At 7:45 p.m., the leader visitors regroup with the Job Seekers in our Fellowship Hall (which also served as our dining room for the dinner) to listen to success stories told by newly hired program grads. Our keynote address follows or an interactive program such as "Ask an Expert" Roundtables, Speed Networking, or a Q and A Panel Discussion. At 9:00 p.m. we bring the program to a close.

RUMC Job Networking Ministry
Program Schedule

1:30 p.m. to 5:30 p.m. - Afternoon workshops

- How to Prepare for an Interview
- Preparing for Difficult Financial Times (Dave Ramsey style training)
- How to Start a Business…is it right for you?
- Maximizing Your Career in Turbulent Times (Crossroads Career Network)
- Specialized training classes as volunteers offer

3:00 p.m. – Church leader visitor meetings

4:30 p.m. - Greeters and set up people begin

5:30 p.m. - Buffet dinner served and guests seated

5:30 p.m. - Table Hosts facilitate guest introductions and networking

6:05 p.m. - Open with prayer

6:15 p.m. - Talk delivered by speaker designed to initiate discussion

6:30 p.m. - Table discussions lead by Table Hosts

6:45 p.m. - General group sharing and closing remarks

6:50 p.m. - Review of choices available for the rest of the meeting

7:00 p.m. - Interactive Sessions and Workshops

- Workshops (currently 3 choices)
- Resume Review
- Industry Guide Program – selection of mentors
- Small Groups Networking by Industry
- Chapel time with pastor, Stephens Ministers, and others

7:45 p.m. - Technical General Session

- Open with prayer
- Announcements
- Success Stories (usually two)
- Keynote address or a Special Interactive Program (i.e.; "Ask an Expert" Roundtables)

8:50 p.m. – Q & A, Closing and Announcements

Promoting the start of new programs:

At the end of the evening, we gather one more time to answer questions and to de-brief our leader visitors. We encourage them to engage the person in their congregation responsible for Job Seeker programs to volunteer with us for a month or more of meetings. The leader then participates in every element of our program.

We also suggest that people who wish to start a program pick one or two parts of our program and simply start, adding additional pieces as each one is fully developed. Jay Litton often reminds us that "if you told me in 1999 that in order to have a successful Job Networking program, I would need a resume review team, I would have never moved ahead!" The secret to success in growth is to build off the strength and gifts of the leaders and volunteers. Given the opportunity, people truly want to serve from their gifts.

Later, we will tell you why we have a resume review team and how that happened. It is an amazing story and one you can easily duplicate!

Dan Guelzo, Reed A. Harvey, Chris Gilliam and Curt Engelmann are just some of the leaders in other churches who visited with us to learn about our programs. They all became volunteers in our ministry and they all went back to their home church to start up career programs. The stories about their experiences are found in Chapter 11.

New Job Networking Ministries

"Is anyone thirsty?
Come and drink—
Even if you have no money!
Come; take your choice of wine or milk—
it's all free!
Why spend your money on food that does
not give you strength?
Why pay for food that does you no good?
Listen to me, and you will eat what is good.
You will enjoy the finest food.
"Come to me with your ears wide open.
Listen and you will find life.
I will make an everlasting covenant with you.
I will give you all the unfailing love
I promised to David".
Isaiah 55:1-3

CHAPTER 2

Developing a Compelling Purpose

We were moving along with our program, since Jay grabbed hold of it in 2000, with just a handful of volunteers, an evening speaker and Industry Guides. Industry Guides (employed church members willing to serve as mentors) volunteer to take telephone calls from Job Seekers in their industry and to assist them in their search. (We will cover the Industry Guide Program in detail in a later section) A database was developed for the Job Seeker attendees and used to email them about future programs. In the formative days we met twice a month from 7:30 p.m. to 9:00 p.m. Pretty simple! At that time, we had a straight forward, professional program designed to encourage Job Seekers and to provide them with quality, technical support.

The speakers came from all over our community. We invited experts in their fields. Rarely would they decline our invitation to speak. They gladly accepted our invitation and each gave his/her best to help the Job Seekers. These business and community leaders spoke on topics such as How to Network, Developing a Resume that Gets Noticed, Best Interviewing Skills, How to Prepare a Job Search, Interviewing with the CEO, Answering Difficult Interview Questions, Establishing Expectations for Time and Challenges, and Using Job Boards. Today, we add to this list, "Ask an Expert" Roundtables and Panel Discussions led by experts in their fields. We also would bring in speakers who talk about Developing Social Media Networking Skills, such as the use of LinkedIn®, Twitter®, and Facebook®.

Our program has always been content driven. Jay finds the best of the best in the community who are willing to share their knowledge on a particular subject. He developed a list of people who know specific topics and will readily share what they know to help Job Seekers. People who are not necessarily "speakers" willingly talk to a group of 50 or 60 about something they know well when they recognize that their wisdom and experience will have a powerful impact on others. Joblessness has touched all of our lives. Either we have been unemployed or we have a friend, family member, or acquaintance going through the job hunting process. We know the pain and the challenges and difficulties the Job Seeker feels and faces. This empathy along with the confidence expressed by being asked to talk about something they know well is often compelling enough to enlist a volunteer speaker.

Our evenings are wrapped in prayer. We begin each program with prayer, end each program with prayer, ask for written, confidential prayer requests, and talk about "keeping God in your search." This reminds us also, that God is in control. It is easy for the volunteers to become discouraged about our inability to help the Job Seekers. Many come to the evening bringing heavy hearts. We must remind ourselves that we are there to offer support, educate, and lend a listening ear. Prayer helps to keep us focused.

People often ask us about the purpose of the program. The purpose is to:

- Reach out to the community;
- Teach valuable job search skills;
- Encourage Job Seekers in their back-to-work journey.

All is accomplished while emphasizing a three point message:

- The search process is difficult;
- You are not alone (look around: peers and caring support abounds);
- This is too difficult to do without God!

We always encourage Job Seekers to claim the resources of our praying church by completing a prayer request card. Job Seekers understand that they have three options to choose from, if they elect to complete a prayer request card:

- Provide their name and phone number on the card and to anticipate a call from our pastor;
- Provide their name on the card and be added to our prayer list which circulates throughout the congregation;
- Choose to be anonymous but be added to the general congregational prayer list.

Although our program has always been content driven, providing solid and practical tools for conducting a job search, there is a consistent message of faith woven into the tapestry of our ministry, that God must be a part of the search process for true success to be realized in the Job Seekers' efforts. Typically, only 5% of our attendees are members of our church. We live in a culturally diverse community drawing to our program people of all faiths and many who have no faith. But, in our program, we try to offer first a full variety of tools and support to help people get back to work and we remain faithful to that objective. However, we are uncompromising in our commitment that we serve a sovereign God who is in charge and involved in our lives. This is the clear message that is delivered by our volunteers through their caring communications and service to the Job Seeker. Please note, that we do not preach or offer an altar call. Our purpose is to demonstrate the compassionate love of God at work in our lives and theirs, simply through our service in this ministry.

Surveys reveal that only 5% of those in attendance are members of our church.

Until 2003, when Resume Review was added, the RUMC Job Networking Ministry consisted basically of only three parts: 1) A warm, friendly greeting; 2) A technical speaker; and 3) The Industry Guides (employed church members willing to serve as mentors). Industry Guides have become so important to the overall program's success that we will devote an entire section to how this effort developed and how it works today. Each evening meeting drew 60 to 80 people from the community twice a month, during good employment times and bad. Clearly, an important community need was being served and God was smiling.

From the beginning, the Job Seekers were a mix of people: our church members, members of other faith communities, no faith affiliation, friends of church members, and people in the community who needed help, support, encouragement and direction. In fact, our informal surveys reveal that only 5% of those in attendance are members of our church. Our volunteers continue to be amazed with how basic and simple developing an outreach such as this truly can be.

As with all dynamic and growing entities, changes occur. This program is no exception. Since the RUMC Job Networking Ministry's inception, we have added resume review, workshops, and a dinner program. The program's purpose and vision were written down by the lay people involved and subsequently anointed through their commitment and participation.

Our purpose has been further clarified as follows:

- To provide a safe and caring place for Job Seekers to be supported in their search, while learning job search skills and process;
- To provide Christian fellowship to Job Seekers, while communicating the need for God's involvement in their search. It is too difficult to do this alone;
- To reach out to those in serious and desperate situations, by not only pointing the way to help, but also providing some of that help;
- To invite people without a church home into the fellowship of believers at RUMC;
- To model a way that the church is relevant in the lives of today's people which is accomplished by providing the Job Seekers with the latest job search knowledge and practices

Job Seekers of the next meeting and program agenda. Email addresses were never dropped unless requested. Even today, the list goes back to the earliest days.

Jay had come to realize something more was needed. What if a Job Seeker could have the personal attention of an employed and caring volunteer to discuss concerns about their job search? Imagine how the Job Seeker would begin to feel supported in this process! The Industry Guide, or mentor, could provide the simple, yet powerful benefit of a listening ear and resource for new ideas to assist the Job Seeker. So Jay decided to solicit help from employed members of our congregation to build the new Industry Guide program.

Sunday morning sharing from the pulpit in 2001 drew many new volunteers to the ministry.

The congregation responded overwhelmingly. Specifically, Jay asked for employed church members who would be willing to accept a phone call from one Job Seeker every two weeks for about 15 minutes to discuss whatever the Job Seeker had on his/her mind. More than 100 people responded that day by providing phone numbers and email addresses. With that initial presentation and request, the Industry Guide Program came into existence. Like all aspects of the Job Seeker ministry, the Industry Guide Program continues growing with the needs of our time. Of all the programs offered, the Industry Guide Program is still one of the most effective ways to provide care and personal support to Job Seekers.

An even greater surprise was the offers of support to the ministry in different areas. A few people offered to review resumes over the telephone. This added a new dimension of support. What a gift these church members provided. This new suggestion was quickly implemented. At the end of each program a volunteer gave a name to each Job Seeker who sought an off-site (by

needed to get the job they want. This also helps spread the word about the program.

The rest of this book not only outlines the "How to" of what is done within this ministry, but it tells the stories of the people involved who make it happen, how God shows up at each meeting, and how these goals play out in both the life of RUMC and in our community.

Be sure to read the stories in Chapter 11 from the volunteers who were part of the program during the formative years. Their experiences will enhance your understanding on how our programs evolved and encourage you by the way each stepped up to serve and was blessed in the process. John Harper, Donna Litton, Neal Reynolds, and Pat Holt joined in the work early and continue to serve today in a variety of new ways, each with a spirit and enthusiasm that motivates both Job Seekers and volunteers.

Developing a Compelling Purpose

- ***John Harper*** ***Page 88***
- ***Donna Litton*** ***Page 93***
- ***Neal Reynolds*** ***Page 96***
- ***Pat Holt*** ***Page 101***

CHAPTER 3

"Which of these...was a neighbor...?
The expert in the law replied,
'The one who had mercy on him.'
Jesus told him, 'Go and do Likewise'"
Luke 10:36-37

Industry Guides and Chocolate Chip Cool

On a Sunday morning in 2001, Jay Litton spoke from the pu
ask the Congregation to support the Job Networking Minist
did not ask for donations. There was no need for money.
from making coffee available, there were basically no ex
However there was a critical need for people - volunteers.

Jay explained that as a result of the extensive dot-com b
failures, combined with the secondary impact of those f
more people were now attending the Job Networking Minist
in previous years. His meager team of volunteers was
strained. This program was offered twice each month
second and fourth Monday evenings. Attendance then
between 60 and 80.

The program operated at that time with very few
volunteers. There were generally four greeters to extend
welcome as each Job Seeker entered. Two more voluntee
needed to staff a table to assist the Job Seekers in registeri
moderated the program and oversaw the content. Fr
beginning of the program, we asked participants to regist
provided a yellow information sheet describing what the
expect during their time with us. A staff member from the
gathered the email addresses, and established a regularly
database of attendees. We used the email database to nc

telephone) resume review. We established the criterion of one Job Seeker per one off-site resume review volunteer.

Soon, one church member asked if he and his wife could make and bring homemade chocolate chip cookies to the meetings. If so, he would make them and deliver them each Monday night that the program met. Of course, we said "Yes, thank you." The chocolate chip cookie baking grew into a family ritual for Sunday afternoons prior to the 2nd and 4th Mondays of the month! Even though the program has grown from 80 Job Seekers and eight volunteers to well over 300 Job Seekers with 100 on site volunteers plus 150 Industry guides. Michael Dubois, his wife Donna, and their six year old daughter continue to make the Chocolate Chip Cookies for the meetings. The story of this family is shared with the Job Seekers each time we meet. Everyone enjoys hearing about this compassionate family and their dedication to help the Job Seekers in their unique way.

A Sunday morning sharing from the pulpit in 2001 drew many new volunteers to the ministry and we moved from having a speaker and a few Industry Guides to a program with much more. In this next step, we added many new Industry Guides, off site resume reviewers and a family providing homemade chocolate chip cookies! Still, the cost of the program was little more than the time contributed freely by the volunteers: the price for a large pot of coffee and a staff person to provide data entry to generate an email blast announcing the next program. In our case, this became a church administration responsibility and it was integrated into other church communications duties.

Be sure to read the story of one Industry Guide, Melton Hood, who answered the call in 2001. He has mentored hundreds of Job Seekers since that day. Read how Gary Shaar expanded the program to what it is today, working from his experience and knowledge base as an executive recruiter. Finally, read the story of personal faith and growth in a young family who spend Sunday afternoon baking chocolate chip cookies for their unemployed neighbors.

Industry Guides and Chocolate Chip Cookies

CHAPTER 4

"As iron sharpens iron,

so one man sharpens another."

Proverbs 27:17

Would You Like to Have Your Resume Reviewed?

The dot-com crash impacted our Job Seekers ministry in other ways. As a business owner in the healthcare staffing industry, our industry saw a massive growth in the number of people seeking placement but were confronted by a lack of job openings. I thought about the Job Networking Ministry at our church and wondered if there was a place for me to use my skills. I attended one of the regular meetings and have been attending, volunteering and participating ever since and that was seven years ago!

This is my story: Toward the end of the evening, Pat Holt, a key volunteer who organized much of the program processes, announced "Off-Site Resume Review" to the Job Seekers. At those words, Job Seekers came forward to receive the name of a volunteer person who had agreed to take a call from a Job Seeker to provide input on his/her resume. I was astounded by the eagerness of the Job Seekers to use this service. Unfortunately, demand for help far exceeded the supply of helpers. My heart ached as I watched so many Job Seekers walk away empty handed. Yet that evening, I asked Pat if I could review a couple of resumes right then, right there.

"Of course! Sit down at a desk and begin," she said. The people who had hoped to receive an off-site resume review sat with me. It was at the end of the evening so there was only time to help two people but the appreciative response of the Job Seekers eased the ache in my heart. And it was such a simple effort on my part!

Before I left the meeting that night, I asked Jay if I could bring a few recruiters with me to the next meeting to engage in on-site resume review. I saw the smile of Jay's face emerge, the smile all of us in this ministry have come to recognize and enjoy. "Yes. Please. Thank you," he said.

I returned for the next meeting with two additional recruiters. We each took a small desk in one of the rooms. A sign announced our presence and new offering of resume review. The Job Seekers thronged to our desks. They grabbed hold of this unique opportunity for one-to-one guidance. A new and vital element to the program had emerged.

My heart ached as I watched so many Job Seekers walk away empty handed.

As the months went by, more recruiters and Human Resource Professionals were added to the now rapidly growing team of Resume Reviewers! We started offering Resume Review as a special part of the program. The recruiters and HR folks arrived at 6:45 p.m., sat one-to-one with Job Seekers, and ended their reviews at 7:30 p.m. This allowed all Job Seekers to proceed to the main program. Recruiting the volunteers to join our resume review team was simple. We asked recruiters and HR people we knew to join us. Then we became really creative and asked job seeking HR professionals who came to the program for the help and support it provided, if they would be willing to help with the resume review. Quickly another dimension emerged – Job Seekers themselves had skills which were vitally needed in our program. Some of them could be volunteers as well as users of the program!

In addition to expanding our outreach and our pool for volunteers, our ministry now had a very ecumenical flavor to it.

Initially, all the volunteers came from our church members. We did not need more than six or seven per meeting to handle the tasks of greeters, organizers and speakers. With the program's growth and the addition of services, this new team came from all walks of life, all areas of town, and with a breadth and dept of backgrounds. The common trait among these volunteers was a willingness to share the skills for which they are paid all day long to help their neighboring Job Seekers attain a more professional resume. One volunteer after another left each meeting knowing that they had helped another person take a significant one step closer to finding employment. These volunteers kept coming back. Soon they were helping each other when there was a need for a job search or networking.

Over time, the resume review portion morphed into an opportunity for the Job Seeker to have a private one-to-one conversation with a professional whose work day consists of interviewing Job Seekers throughout the day. The volunteers shared honestly with the Job Seekers about such things as professional dress, handling difficult situations as it pertains to their history on a resume, use of job boards in their search, and much more. Conversation among our resume review volunteers helped us recognize that Job Seekers 50 years of age and above consistently wondered how much job history to include on their resume. We looked at ways to provide additional help and support to these uniquely qualified and experienced individuals.

Job Seekers themselves had skills which were vitally needed in our program.

As the ministry grew in number of volunteers and Job Seekers, we realized the need to provide nurture for the volunteers by hosting a few social gatherings. On meeting nights the volunteers frequently arrived, did their part and then departed, never having the time to talk to each other. Since some volunteers now came from outside of our congregation, few really got to know each other. Our first social gathering was held at a restaurant with 20 people during the Christmas holiday season. We quickly saw how much the group enjoyed getting to know one another. We were struck by a blinding flash of the obvious: we were forming a Team and had not realized it.

Today the resume review list of volunteers is 50 people long with approximately 20 in attendance at each meeting. They devote an hour to reviewing resumes and in that hour, each volunteer speaks one-to-one with three or four Job Seekers. We constantly add new volunteers to the team. Meanwhile the off-site resume review continues and has grown as well. A few of our volunteers are managers and owners of companies where they build teams, are responsible for hiring and see many resumes. These volunteers bring practical experience to the Job Seekers as they review the Job Seeker's resume. The entire Resume Review Team talks to approximately 65 Job Seekers in one evening. Even while the Job Seekers wait on line for their turn, one of our volunteers, Eric West, provides coaching and training, job skills and search techniques that can help the Job Seeker move forward. Eric's actual duty as a volunteer is to help guide Job Seekers along the line to the next available person ready to help with a resume review. But, Eric, in all his creativity, has formulated a way to help people while they wait. He conducts an informal question and answer time for all who will listen...and by the way...he does it with humor. I often hear and see the people on line laughing and having fun. No time goes unutilized!

In Chapter 11, Stories from the Volunteers, Nancy Schrempp addresses the need to encourage the volunteers. A few social gatherings each year go a long way in developing relationships among this committed team. Barbara Marks now leads the Resume Review team and enjoys letting us know how much this event touches the community. How she became a volunteer is an amazing story. Craig Simons is a dedicated resume review volunteer who speaks to how much the individual reviews with Job Seekers has lead to personal growth for himself. Eric's story is such an inspiration on how one can make the job of handling the queue of waiting Job Seekers into a time of both learning and fun.

Would You Like to Have Your Resume Reviewed?

CHAPTER 5

"'For I know the plans I have for you, declares the lord, plans to prosper you and not to harm you, plans to give you hope and a future."

Jeremiah 29:11

Build It and They Will Come

My first meeting was in 2003. Earlier, we discussed that this now successful Job Seeker ministry began in the early 90's at the impetus of one individual. The intent was to provide encouragement and support to those who were between jobs and actively seeking a new job. Attendance was sparse but the dedication of the leader was huge, and he persevered. When Jay attended his first Job Seeker gathering as a volunteer in 1997 only one person was present other than himself. Jay's story appears in Chapter 10. By the time I arrived for my first meeting in the fall of 2003, approximately 50 people were attending Job Networking at a regular meeting. That evening, one of the leaders asked for a show of hands from those who were attending for the first time. About half of these people raised their hands. Amazingly, this pattern persists. With over 40 Job Networking programs available in the metro-Atlanta area, nearly 50% of those in attendance at our meetings are there for the first time. It is unclear if there is something to learn from this fact, but what we do know is that the ministry continues to touch new lives and by extension new families every time it meets.

We began maintaining an official database of attendees in 2000. We have continued, since that time, to keep two separate sign-in lists at each meeting. One list is for those who have attended the meetings before. The Job Seekers are asked to find their name and to make sure that their email information is correct. The other list is for those who are there for the first time. The repeat participants actually appreciate seeing their name on the list! Someone cares enough to keep track of them. They are a part of the group. No one's name is ever removed from the contact list unless the individual asks that we do so. In this way, we continue to remain connected with those we served and those who served, years after our time together.

This database is our primary tool for maintaining contact with current and former Job Seekers. Several days prior to the next meeting, an email is sent to inform them about the upcoming program. The email contains a detailed announcement about the featured speaker, the speaker's topic and how the topic will assist the Job Seekers in their job hunting and Job Networking. We remind our attendees of other programs available (Resume Review, Industry Guide, workshops, etc.) We have discovered that former Job Seekers, who are now employed, forward the email to their friends who are unemployed.

Today individuals are learning that whether working or out of work, it is essential to remain actively in networking in order to minimize the consequences of being out of work. Some attendees participate in the meetings because they want to be ahead of the curve, concerned that they may be in the next round of layoffs or staff reductions. Others attend because they have chosen to begin to look for other employment while they still hold a job. What is true in our area is true everywhere. Whatever reason brings an individual to a Job Seeker meeting, the result is the same. Today's fluid employment situation generates an ongoing need for programs that can coach people in the process of the job search, while assisting Job Seekers to meet others who may be connected to the job they want next.

The need for a career focused program such as we see today will never disappear, even when our unemployment situation improves. Participants' names stay on our database in order to maintain their connection with us. They want to be informed. They want to pass the word on to others. They want to know what is going on in the employment community. They want to attend the meetings. Different reasons for career transition will always exist. In our program, volunteers and speakers teach networking skills and emphasize the importance of continuing the process of building one's own personal professional database.

To date, our database contains over 4,000 current email addresses. A church staff member enters the newly obtained email addresses while the internal system corrects for bounce backs and requests for removals.

Today's fluid employment situation generates an ongoing need for programs that can coach people in the process of the job search.

As the ministry grew, we recognized the importance of building a website just for the Job Seeker program. The website undergoes periodic updates and revisions. We want the information provided on the website to be current, informative and helpful. Each email blast that goes out to every person in the database reminds the recipients to check out the website for more information on the program in particular and on the job networking scene in general. This website also provides a means for Job Seekers to connect into the Crossroads Career Network®. To complete the connection on line with Crossroads, Job Seekers must have a password. We provide that password when they attend our Job Networking meeting. (See Chapter 6 "Getting Connected" to learn more about Crossroads)

We also maintain an active Yahoo! ® Groups account. Employers post job openings on our account and other networking groups announce their meeting times and locations. Job Seekers registered with our program can choose to receive a daily digest of announcements. This Yahoo!® Group page is another great way for us to stay connected with the Job Seekers and to reach them quickly with opportunities. In addition, we have developed an

RUMC LinkedIn® group for those who wish to sign up. This tool requires a volunteer to manage the process, but these tools are the answer to the most frequently asked question, "How do you get the word out about your programs?" We continue to re-evaluate and add more ways to communicate as we discover them and have the volunteers to manage the process.

Read in Chapter 11 how Kay Holmquist tells about her involvement as a church staff member handling communications for the ministry. Darren Shipp tells the difficult and rewarding story of how after moving his family to our community for a job change, he found himself part of another "cut-back" and how he was lead to the Job Networking through the pastoral staff. These stories provide an interesting perspective on the impact of church staff in these ministries.

Build It and They Will Come

- ***Darren Shipp*** ***Page 132***
- ***Kay Holmquist*** ***Page 136***

Development of RUMC Job Networking Ministry

1989 – 2000

- Semi-monthly program was led by volunteers who would talk to Job Seekers on subjects as requested and review their resume.

2000 – 2003

- Under new leadership, new volunteer leaders added and started guest speaker program started, teaching key elements of the search process
- Industry Guide Program created-recruited over 110 new volunteers
- New focus on Prayer

2004 - 2007

- On-site resume review introduced-delivered by executive recruiters and human resource professionals
- Prayer request cards added to be distributed to prayer team via email and Sunday worship attendees via prayer sheet.
- Off-site resume review added
- Introduced new technical programs in addition to guest speakers: "Ask An Expert" Roundtables and "Panel of Experts" discussions

2008

- Faith Based dinner program added – dinner served at tables of eight, hosted by table facilitator volunteers, a guest speaker and table discussions.

2009

- New Workshops: Interviewing Skills, Start Your Own Business and Resume Writing
- Small Group Networking program: organized by Industry and Profession
- Chapel time: a volunteer prayer team offering individual prayers over Job Seekers

2010

- LinkedIn Profiles Review: added as a compliment to Resume Reviews

CHAPTER 6

"Stand at the Crossroads and look...

find rest for your soul."

Jeremiah 6:16

Getting Connected!

In 2006, our church joined Crossroad Careers® Network, led by Brian Ray and his wife, Kristy. Becoming part of Crossroads opened up a whole new world of connections, resources, and opportunities. We had a network of churches with which we could share ideas to improve our programs and be with other people who are interested and passionate about helping people find the right employment fit.

Brian Ray is an Executive Recruiter and has years of history with Job Seekers and employers. Since my history includes owning a healthcare staffing company for many years, our paths crossed at Conferences and other events focusing on business growth and serving to all of our clients. Brian became passionate about defining the search process: ways a Job Seeker can begin to plan to search for the next career opportunity. Over many years Brian developed a program that defined each step in an organized and thoughtful process. He created and made resources available and named his creation: Crossroads Career® Network. The ministry focuses upon following God's plan for one's life. The program and materials assist Job Seekers to incorporate this very same thinking into their pursuit of the next right career choice.

Crossroads enables us to have a powerful connection with other faith communities and Job Networking ministries. Being successfully connected always requires a mutual covenant. People of faith know and understand the significance of covenant. In this particular setting, the connection or covenant provides access for us to many additional resources and great ideas! We in turn, as part of our Job Networking Ministry, connect our Job Seekers to all the materials and programs Crossroads makes available on their website as well as at his yearly conferences. This is an enormously valuable resource for Job Seekers and for any Job Networking Ministry. The content of the program can best be told by the founder, Brian Ray and by Peter Bourke, who has used this material to build a wonderfully successful Job Seeker program that meets weekly at North Point Community Church in Alpharetta, Georgia. Their stories follow:

(The following article is excerpted and adapted from Brian Ray's article: *Churches Helping People through Crossroads in their Careers*. Used by permission of the author.)

Churches Helping People Through Crossroads in their Careers

By Brian Ray, Founder, Crossroads Career© Network
www.CrossroadsCareer.org

As I write this, more than half of the 150+ million people in the U.S. workforce are unemployed, underemployed, miserably-employed or nervously-employed. The economy is causing a roller coaster ride for millions. The nature of employment is changing. Workers are finding themselves at a career crossroads, forced into career transitions with little or no help navigating the process.

Helping people navigate their career crossroads, by connecting them to Christ, is an awesome ministry opportunity for churches.

Janet King in Snellville, Georgia writes of her career crossroads experience:

"My boss gave me the news that the customer for my main project decided not to buy from us and so my salary could not be justified any longer. I fumed, I panicked, I cried! I felt as if I had been traveling along (in my career) when the bus stopped, the door opened and I was pushed out – at a crossroads – and I felt abandoned."

After going through a Crossroads Career® workshop at Snellville United Methodist Church, Janet is working as a contractor for her former employer, and she is volunteering in the Crossroads Career Network Ministry at Snellville United Methodist Church:

"I'm working like crazy these days; my boss has a big project. I taught the Crossroads Career® class tonight and it was lots of fun, as always!"

Job Seekers and career explorers are gaining more than career guidance through Crossroads Career® workshops, their lives are changing. Many are becoming volunteers, like Janet, using their talents and interests as marketplace ministers.

More Churches are interested in Job/Career Ministry:

"A February 2009 Lifeway Research survey of 1,000 Protestant churches nationwide found that 31 percent were considering creating or expanding ministries for the unemployed. 62 percent had been approached for help by persons from their community, while 31 percent had been approached by their own church members." (September 2, 2009, ChristianityToday.Com)

The Crossroads Career® Network (CCN) is a national membership of churches providing practical, comprehensive career resources to thousands of Job Seekers and career explorers. For some churches, CCN is a community outreach and evangelism ministry, for others; discipleship and stewardship. Yet, all CCN churches consider job/career ministry as an opportunity to help and care for others with Christ's love.

How to Start and Grow a Job/Career Ministry:

"Don't reinvent the wheel," as many of our ministry leaders say. CCN will equip your church for an effective Christ-centered job/career ministry.

For a $600 annual subscription, your church has unlimited 24/7 access to career, ministry and employer resources available online at: www.CrossroadsCareer.org.

Through CCN, your church will be able to:

- Support Job Seekers and career explorers to find jobs, career, calling;
- Equip volunteers to minister to Seekers and explorers;
- Help local employers to find candidates.

Additionally, your subscription includes on-the-ground ministry help, national and local conferences, and an exclusive Crossroads Career Network LinkedIn group for ministry leaders and teams to communicate and collaborate.

Getting Connected!

The heart of the CCN resource kit is the 2010 Crossroads Career Workbook *"Maximize Your Career,"* featuring six key steps to find jobs, careers and calling.

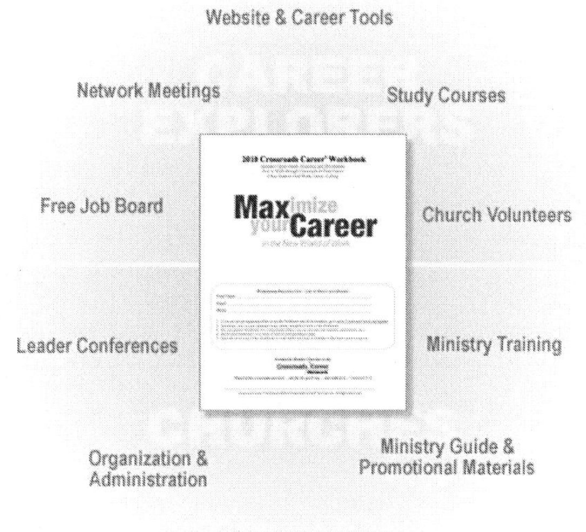

More than 100 executives and experts in human resources, recruiting, career coaching, job search, resume writing, and training and development contributed to this workbook and its online resources.

The workbook includes a career guide, work exercises and read-and-write devotionals. While Job Seekers/career explorers can complete the workbook on their own, it is even better to for them to get together with others in a small group or workshop.

Additional online resources include career transition and discover-your-calling tools:

- Free online assessment of your God-given gifts;
- The web's largest job search engine;
- Online resume building service.

1) Start with Crossroads Career Website

You can immediately help members in your congregation and community. Provide them access to our wealth of online job search tools and career-related materials, including local employer job postings.

2) Build a Ministry Team

After you launch your website ministry, you can recruit volunteers and equip them with already-prepared ministry guides and materials to begin an effective in-person ministering environment for Job Seekers and career explorers.

Your church can select from a variety of ministry guides, materials and tools to support a selection of ministry environments:

- Weekly support groups for encouragement and networking;
- Monthly job-networking meetings with speakers;
- Job search and career workshops;
- Small group study courses;
- One-to-one career coaching and mentoring;
- Employer involvement programs like career fairs.

There are also prayer and publicity resources to help you promote CCN to Job Seekers, as well as recruit and equip volunteers.

3) Already have a Career Ministry? Want More Resources?

Use Crossroads Career resources to pump even more life into your existing ministry. CCN provides continuously-updated career resources, as well as ministry guides, tools and materials for every aspect of your ministry. Use your own ministry name, or the Crossroads Career® name.

How and why did I get involved in job/career ministry?

The idea of helping people through job/career transition came to me in 1985 when I was VP for HR and Administration at Chick-fil-A. We had 10,000 people a year inquiring about staff or operator opportunities, yet we could choose only 100. I wondered what positive influence we might have on the 9,900 inquirers who did not get chosen.

Initial meetings with Christian business people sparked some interest, but nothing really gelled. A couple of years later, I helped a recruiter and an outplacement executive start a Christian coaching placement ministry called Crossroads Career Services, Inc., but it did not last.

By 1990, I had started a retained executive search consulting business serving a handful of employers. At the same time, I encouraged a group of individuals who were hungry to seek real success, something with meaning and purpose, more than just another job and paycheck.

I will never forget an executive named John. One evening, he showed up early for our weekly networking meeting and asked, "Can we pray? I am not really comfortable with the whole praying thing, but it seems OK here." Wow! Talk about opportunity to move from felt need to real need. People weren't just finding jobs, they were finding Jesus. They weren't just making career transitions; they were being transformed by Christ!

Over the years, the group out grew our little conference room, so I asked my local church if we could meet in a room at the church. The founders of Crossroad Career Services gave me permission to use the brand name for our meetings. At our first meeting, we had four volunteers and three attendees. A year later, we hosted our first all-day career conference – 40 volunteers and 435 attendees. Within a year, two more churches had started Crossroads Career ministries, and a third church wanted their own ministry.

God's Vision or My Hallucination?

Near the end of 1999, one of my friends asked, "What if you took a year off, and devoted it to developing and launching a network of churches with career ministries?" My response, "Ohhh, let me pray about that!"

Well, pray I did and as a result believed that I should set aside up to three years to start the network, so long as God would provide. In year one of the three-year plan, a working, self-sustaining, replicable program would be developed. Year two, we would launch into a variety of Atlanta-area churches. Year three was included in my plan in case things got a slow start. January 2000 was the official start, but it took a few months to wind down my business, and hand it off to others.

I think it was July when I made my first fundraising call. I phoned one of my (former) clients – a Christian owner of a venture capital firm – who knew what I was doing. He started telling me about his private foundation and that I should send a proposal to the executive director. I started not feeling so good. "Ok," I said. Then he said, "Do you remember the training consulting business you worked on? We sold part of that, and I will send you a check for your share." "OKAY!" I said. The next day UPS delivered an envelope with a check that provided for the first year costs of this ministry!

God also provided free office space, furniture, computers, equipment, and phone service the first year. We developed the program and test drove it successfully in two churches, and even added a third church that wanted a Crossroads Career Ministry. We were ahead of schedule! And, the first edition of the Crossroads Career workbook was published.

In the second year we joined a ministry that helped start-up ministries and began our effort to launch into more churches. God provided two key employees, an expanded board, and 15 more churches. I learned lots; the most important lesson was this: this ministry is not mine; it is God's. I get to help.

In May of the third year (2002), I returned to business. I continue to volunteer, some years more than others and do my best to hear and follow God's calling.

Getting Connected!

Last year, the number of churches in the Crossroads Career Network grew nation-wide from 41 to 127. Over 500 volunteers served thousands of Job Seekers and career explorers.

Over the years, the one verse that has been our beacon for helping others is Jeremiah 6:16:

This is what the LORD says:

"Stand at the crossroads and look; ask for the ancient paths, ask where the good way is, and walk in it, and you will find rest for your souls..."

Crossroads Career® Network

How can your church find out more?

Please sign-up for a free 15-day trial membership to see and explore all the resources.

Just go to **www.CrossroadsCareer.org/freetrial.** If you have questions, please email me at brian@CrossroadsCareer.org.

Brian Ray:

I am a volunteer and founder of Crossroads Career® Network, a national membership of 100+ churches equipped to help people find jobs, careers, and calling. My business experience includes owner of Primus Consulting executive search and consulting firm, and Vice President for Human Resources and Administration for Chick-fil-A restaurant chain. I am married to Kristy, and together we have four children and seven grandchildren. We are living in Charlotte NC, and are members of Transformation Church.

The Story of C3G

Over the past few years, I have personally witnessed the job searches of several hundred people. I've seen the good, the bad, and, in more cases than I would care to admit, even the ugly. I've interviewed and hired hundreds of people over the course of my corporate career. I've seen about every conceivable job search approach and scenario.

In 2003, I devoted six months to finding out where God wanted me to spend my time and energy in alignment with His will and the gifts and experiences God had blessed me with. I had a clear sense that my calling was related to the field of career transition because of my experience in the industry and the obvious fact that so many people struggle immensely and painfully with career transitions. In fact, I recognized that career-related challenges create a unique "life-crisis" situation in which many people become more inclined to ask hard, faith-related questions and become more receptive to finding (or strengthening) their relationship with Jesus in the process. As a friend of mine once said, "When we become unemployed, it's as though God has figured out that the only way we tend to look up towards heaven is when He knocks us on our back."

In my typical, Type "A" fashion, I interviewed over 200 people who were either unemployed or misemployed. I also spoke with a large number of career counselors or ministry leaders who were dedicated to helping people with career transition challenges. I even interviewed the spouses of many career explorers. I focused on learning, helping where possible, and perhaps most importantly, determining where God wanted me to contribute. I wasn't sure if I was supposed to make my living in this arena or be involved as an avocation and find another way to pay the bills.

I quickly recognized that this was not the ideal way for me to try to make a living – I'm blessed to be able to do that with a small sales training and consulting organization. Equally obvious to me were opportunities for me to contribute, and through the Grace of God and the experience of the last seven years, I've developed some observations and recommendations about what works and what's missing for people in the career search process today.

It's a simple approach called Christ Centered Career Groups (C3G) and it combines the power of a small group of Christians doing "life" together with the needs of people who are either unemployed or employed workers actively looking for new (or better) employment.

Here's a parallel: Many large churches have been creating a way to bring members into closer relationships by developing small group programs. In essence, they create a forum for six to eight adults or couples in a similar stage of life (age, location, children, etc.) to "do life" together in a Christ-centered way. They often meet weekly to build relationships, to help each other in a variety of circumstances, and to learn and study the Bible together. These groups provide members with support, genuine care, and even accountability in a variety of life's circumstances.

We've learned that this same small group approach can be effectively applied to those going through career transition. If a person struggling with unemployment or searching for a better career alternative can find three to six other people who are willing to commit to walk the journey together and to stay together as a team until all of the group members find work, it will significantly enhance their individual (and collective) effectiveness in the process.

When initiated properly, the small group becomes a powerful forum for people to get practical, spiritual, and emotional support. It's an effective way to share lessons learned and great ideas, a means of holding each other accountable, and, ultimately, a forum to show others the love of Christ at a critical time in their life. This C3G concept was piloted and developed in Alpharetta, Georgia in collaboration with Northpoint Community Church (www.northpoint.org/jobhelp) and has been integrated into the broader Crossroads Career™ Network (www.crossroadscareer.org) tools we make available to churches in the U.S. who want to start or enhance their own career ministry.

The job search process is a very lonely time for most people, perhaps even more so for men (we tend to be less "relational") but certainly not exclusively. Most Career Explorers, as we call them in the Crossroads Career Network Ministry, feel as though they're alone and on their own during career transition. In their previous jobs, they'd have a team of people working with them. They had regular meetings with their manager to report on progress and could ask for input and feedback on projects and activities. They always felt like they were part of a bigger organization where they could make a contribution, where people would help each other, where they could develop personal and professional relationships, and even celebrate successes.

The job search environment is entirely different. Most people have very little interaction with anyone outside of their direct family unless it's an all-too-occasional phone call or cup of coffee with a friend during the networking process. The Career Explorers feel pressure from all relationship sides—kids, spouse, and parents—although much of the pressure for the average person is self-imposed. The Career Explorers often admit to severe bouts of lost confidence. Some are honest enough to admit they're depressed (although very few actually do anything about it). Except for some displaced workers who may have the benefit of working with an outplacement firm, Job Seekers are largely left to fend for themselves.

Yet, the vast majority of us are not well-equipped to search for work effectively. Some find resources at the Department of Labor's local unemployment office while they file for benefits.

Many spend the vast majority of their time combing the Internet job boards and submitting resumes to the open positions that interest them. The average person who loses his/her job is far from an expert on how to find a new one. Just as a working person has a plan to achieve their objectives, anyone looking for a job needs a plan - a strategy that has proven to be successful. The Job Seeker still struggles, "How do I learn how to search effectively?" They don't have outplacement help; they don't have the money to pay a career counselor; and most often they don't even know where to start!

Perhaps most importantly, Job Seekers, even Christian ones, tend to make another job search mistake: leaving God out of the whole equation. In the same way we tend to compartmentalize God when things are going well in our work (and in our life for that matter), we're often guilty of the same attitude in career transition. I've heard people say, "I'm too busy finding a job to spend time with God." Or "God hasn't delivered a new job yet, why should I count on Him going forward?" God doesn't want to be left out when we're working nor does God want to be left out when we're not.

It's precisely these challenges that Christ Centered Career Groups (C3G) are designed to help a Career Explorer overcome. Their purpose is to provide practical, emotional, and spiritual support to the unemployed participants through weekly, two-hour small group meetings that facilitate prayer, relationship development, encouragement, individual and group accountability, and an opportunity for service by loving friends. One unique aspect of this program is that when a small group is formed, the members are encouraged to commit, via a written covenant, to staying together until all members of the group are employed. I know that makes many who read this pause – "Am I really prepared to make **that** kind of commitment?"

Roswell United Methodist Church and its Job Networking Ministry and volunteers clearly demonstrate a willingness to make the commitment necessary to provide a powerful and effective ministry. C3G is proud to be partnered with RUMC Job Networking in this effort.

Peter Bourke;

I am the volunteer leader of the Christ Centered Career Group (C3G) ministry at Northpoint Community Church in Alpharetta, Georgia I have also served the Crossroads Career Network Board since 2004. My "tent making" is as a Principal for The Complex Sale, a sales training and consulting firm. I am married to Devonie for nearly 30 years and we have three grown daughters and a grandson due to arrive in April, 2010!

I can be reached at pbourke@complexsale.com

CHAPTER 7

"Then their eyes were opened and they recognized him"
Luke 24:31

Keeping God in Your Search

By the end of 2007, our nation's economic condition slid swiftly into a recession, the depth of which we had not experienced since the Great Depression. Economic forecasts suggest that in the near term future the United States is likely to see continued unemployment beyond 10%.

At every meeting we always remind the Job Seekers and the volunteers that "Being out of work is too hard to go it alone! You must keep God in your search!"

In the early years of this ministry, 2000-2003, we would begin each meeting at 7:30 pm, with a welcome by the ministry leader. Then we would introduce the man who best represents the loving theme of our ministry through the warmth of how he greets every attendee. John Harper is a retired executive and senior member of our church. John begins each meeting with a heartfelt prayer. John has a unique gift in recognizing the painful issues that being out of work exacts upon an individual and the family. The issues extend beyond loss of income and impact family lifestyle and decisions. His prayers touched the hearts of us all while lifting those hurts and hopes to our compassionate, loving God. His prayers continue to inspire everyone.

We also have always given each attendee the opportunity to experience the full power of prayer by submitting a prayer request card. Each card will receive the highest level of corporate prayer from our prayer team and our congregation. These prayer requests are added to our prayer list, which is received by our designated prayer team and distributed in worship on Sundays. Those who have shared their telephone numbers on the prayer request card receive a call from our pastor of Membership Care. These phone calls provide an amazing outreach to the community from our church.

As noted earlier, only 5% of the Job Seekers attending our programs are actually members of our church. Imagine receiving a phone call from a pastor at the church you attended the day before for a career program and having that pastor ask, " How are you?", "How can we help you?", "How is your family?", "Can I pray for you?" This is a simple outreach of caring and faith…truly following Jesus' calling to care for his "sheep."

The emotional issues associated with job loss and unemployment had grown to infect many other areas of their lives.

As the economic conditions worsened, unemployment grew and attendance at our meetings grew as well. Now we had people attending our sessions who had never imagined being unemployed much less actually living from an unemployment check. Many of these individuals had not interviewed for jobs since they left high school or college graduation and had been terminated after many years of employment at the same company. We began to see depression and pain in the eyes of so many of the Job Seekers. Our program needed something different, a new element.

For most of the years we have been offering this ministry, 90% of our attendees have been male, over 40, middle to upper income professionals. Conversations among Job Seekers focused on finding a new opportunity. Emotional or personal discussions were limited. Little was shared about the painful and fearful experiences surrounding unemployment. We recognized that the time had come to address the deep seated and numbing pains and fears.

The conversation I had with the human resources professional, which I shared at the beginning of this book, provided the epiphany that launched our next step. The human resources professional related that his friend felt no longer respected by his wife since he had been out of work for six months. This was merely the tip of the iceberg for all the other issues that churned internally for the friend and the friend's wife. We recognized that this couple was not only engaged in the struggles surrounding the job search, but that the emotional issues associated with job loss and unemployment had grown to infect many other areas of their lives. We challenged ourselves to identify a process or provide a comfortable environment where hurting people could meet with others to share and provide emotional support for each other.

Providing a dinner program prior to our existing program became the answer. We believed that sharing a meal, in small groups of eight seated at roundtables that are covered with white tablecloths (not paper), hosted by a sensitive caring group leader would be the answer. By offering a directed faith-based message in combination with a caring facilitator, we believed we could create an environment that would encourage people to speak about the pain of being out of work and to hear how others are dealing with it. We were correct and the response was overwhelming.

We launched our first dinner June 9, 2008 with 64 Job Seekers in attendance plus 15 volunteer leaders and servers. The Job Seekers who came to the dinner stayed for the 7:30 p.m. program, where they were joined by another 120 Job Seekers who came for our speaker and our other technical programs. Today, we typically serve dinner to 275 Job Seekers with an additional 20 to 30 Job Seekers coming after dinner for the remaining program.

Our format is simple. We call our dinner portion "Developing Your Spiritual Resume." Our dinners have always been offered free to the Job Seekers as the meals were funded by a few donations to the ministry by both corporate businesses in our community and personal donations. As the number of dinner participants grew, we had some of the Job Seekers offering to donate towards the cost of the meal. We also found that the meals were far more successful, popular and helpful than we had anticipated. For the sake of the ministry and to honor those who wanted to contribute in some fashion, we started accepting donations from Job Seekers. A simple hand drawn sign now suggests a donation of $3.00, for those who care to give.

Receiving the blessings of Pastor Mike, along with his encouragement and endorsement, we were ready to "rock and roll!"

To date, our dinner program is completely funded by volunteer, private, and corporate donations. Two church members organized an amazing Garage Sale in August 2009. Over 200 church members volunteered to assist in the adventure that raised $15,500 for the Job Networking Ministry. That money combined with the average evening donation received from the Job Seekers for the cost of food will fully fund the dinners through 2010 as long as we don't encounter any unforeseen changes! Our church kitchen staff prepares simple, hot meals that are expandable should more arrive than planned (two nights we had 450 in attendance with 375 joining us for dinner! What a surprise!).

From the conception of the dinner idea until its launch three months passed. There were several meetings during this time with our Senior Pastor, Mike Long, seeking his approval to continue planning this event. He encouraged us to continue to lay out the details. Those words were music to our ears! During those months, I worked to convince others that the logistics were not insurmountable, that we could find funding and that it would serve as a vital support for the Job Seekers. Several months were spent in determining a format for the dinners. One of our RUMC lay leaders, Rusty Gordon, has a tremendous amount of experience organizing and speaking at the 10 year old High Tech Prayer Breakfast by High Tech Ministries now popular all over the

Atlanta area. Rusty invited us to his office on several occasions to share the format used at these breakfasts, how it was achieved and why. He offered to support our dinner ministry when we inaugurated it. We accepted his offer and asked him not only to be the first dinner speaker but also to do a series of talks.

A close friend and former employee at RUMC, Mary Schaefer, played a key role in planning the flow of the event, hot meals that could work within our budget, and worked through the process that was needed to schedule details with the church staff. Receiving the blessings of Pastor Mike, along with his encouragement and endorsement, we were ready to "rock and roll!" Today, Mary is involved in every decision that is made, leads the volunteer team for Table Hosts, and hosts a table for Job Seekers at each meeting.

Our initial Table Host team was handpicked from our congregation. We picked people who we knew could be counted on to be committed to the Job Seekers, were spiritually sound, wanted the program to succeed, and were involved in our church in many ways. We called them our "Dream Team" and felt that if the dinner program did not work it would not be because we had the wrong people. Without exception all of the people on the Dream Team said "yes" to the call when asked to be a Table Host. There was and is no homework, no preparation, no training needed for this group of volunteers. We stressed in the invitation to serve as Table Host that everything they did in their lives and every Sunday School Lesson they had taught or participated in and every sermon they ever heard would be all the preparation they would need to be great!

We set up 10 round tables set to seat eight people. Jay announced the dinner at the previous meeting, on the database program announcement, in the church bulletin, on the yahoo groups email, and at other church programs which he attends and participates. We planned dinner for 80; 79 people showed up (including the volunteers)! The next dinner, the same thing happened again: planned for 80 and 79 showed up! The third time, we set 14 tables of eight, prepared for 112. You guessed it ...110 showed up! Wow! God was all over this plan!

After three dinners, we met with the Table Hosts to talk about what was going right, what needed changing and what could be added. The excitement was high. Near the end of the conversation, one of the Table Hosts said, "Maybe we should start having RSVP. What if we run out of food?" The conversation went in all directions around the room. We considered everything from people feeling they could not attend because they had not RSVP'd earlier to not having enough food. After all the thoughts were shared and a lot of discussion had gone on, quiet descended upon us. Finally someone spoke, "The first meeting we prepared for 80, 79 showed up. At the second meeting, the same results were seen. At the third dinner meeting we prepared for 112 and 110 showed up. Seems like God got the numbers right three times in a row! I wonder what God is thinking now as He listens to this conversation?" That was and has been the very last conversation we have ever had about calling for an RSVP! To date, we have never run out of food.

Following the dinner, at the 7:30 program we told the Job Seekers the story about how God showed up at the dinners and how He "got the number right." The group of 180 in attendance that night roared with laughter and clapped. What a testimony this was to how God is in the details.

The dinner format has gone through many tweaks and changes as we learned how to accommodate a larger attendance. The basics are still present:

- Greeters at the door with big welcomes;
- Table for donations;
- Greeters for seating Job Seekers completely filling front tables first;
- Servers serving food buffet style (managing portions);
- Program
  - Open with a welcome;

- Opening Prayer;
- Speaker on a topic that is relevant to Job Seekers and focused on faith during difficult times (approx 15 minutes);
- Each Table Host distributes information on the evening activities, along with a simple card containing a Bible verse and questions related to the speaker's talk. This card is used to prompt subsequent table discussions;
- Table Discussion on the speaker's talk which is lead by the Table Host using the questions on the card (approx 15 minutes);
- General group sharing of insights from the table discussions and a Closing summary;
- Announcements and a review of the remaining program options with instructions.

The dinner portion of the program ends at 7:00 p.m. At the tables, the Job Seekers sign-in on the provided sign-in sheets, receive name tags, receive printed cards with Bible Verse and questions related to the speaker's talk, are introduced to the other table mates, and are given information sheets about the evening's schedule including how to sign up with Crossroads, Yahoo!® Groups, other ministry opportunities and more;

Today our volunteers come from our church and the community. At least one third of all our Table Hosts now come from area churches. These new Table Hosts are recommended to us from our existing member Table Hosts.

The Table Hosts take home copies of the sign-in sheets which they use to write notes to the Job Seekers at their tables. The notes are full of encouragement and invitations to sit with them and their families in church any Sunday. Often the notes include a special job related devotional. A few of the Table Hosts share their messages with us and we distribute them to the others. Seeing what other Table Hosts share in their notes helps save writing time each week that we meet. Everything is done by email. Sometimes a Table Host may offer to meet with a Job Seeker for coffee and conversation. The Table Hosts are amazingly committed people who feel that they are making a difference and answering a calling at a special and rather fragile time of life for the Job Seekers.

Do not miss the heart warming stories in Chapter 11 from the volunteers in this segment of the ministry. Currently there are about 50 Table Hosts on Mary Schaefer's volunteer team, with 35 in attendance at any given meeting. Read Mary's story about the joy of growing and serving with this little army. Read stories of Table Hosts who have become dinner speakers and of volunteer couples who work together in this ministry. Read from Roger and Gale who have enlisted an entire serving team by getting their Sunday school class engaged in the ministry. Read about the impact of volunteers praying with Job Seekers. You cannot help but be moved by these volunteer stories.

Keeping God in Your Search

CHAPTER 8

"And He has given us this command: Whoever loves God must also love his brother."
1 John 4: 21

Would You Like to Deliver a Keynote Address?

With both a dinner speaker and another speaker at 7:45 p.m., we began calling our later program guest our Keynote Speaker. Speakers for our programs are carefully selected and are truly professionals in a specific area. They may be an expert on Netweaving, the interview process, the steps needed to prepare for the interview, how to use today's social media such as LinkedIn®, Facebook®, and Twitter® and other work related topics. Many of these speakers deliver their messages at career transition programs all over the Greater Atlanta Area. They are professional and well prepared.

Job Seekers walk away from these Keynote talks with useful information they can use the next day in their search preparation. Most of the speakers own or work in businesses that teach or use the material taught in these 45 minute presentations. Often they are recruiters or own search firms, or are employed as Human Resource Managers and Directors. Many of the speakers have written a book that they are willing to sell at cost or give away. (It is important to mention that 80% of our workshop leaders and resume review team come from the community and are not members of our church.)

Occasionally we vary this portion of the program. Instead of a speaker, we will present:

- "Ask an Expert" Roundtable Discussions;
- Panel of Experts (usually three);

- Speed Networking.

These programs are truly fun and interactive. In preparation for roundtables and speed networking we suggest in the announcement that the Job Seekers come prepared with business cards/contact business cards from contacts they make!

80% of our workshop leaders and resume review team come from the community and are not members of our church.

Ask an Expert Roundtables utilizes our very own Resume Review Team and Workshop Leaders (soon to be discussed). We invite between 10 and 12 professionals to lead a roundtable on a topic they know best. These topics may include:

- How to Prepare Your Search;
- Best Ways to Work with Human Resources;
- Getting the Most from Job Boards;
- How to Network and Where;
- How to Prepare for the Interview;
- How to Answer Difficult Interview Questions;
- How to Prepare Your 30 Second "Elevator" speech;
- The WOW Presentation: a unique interview process that gets results.

There is no limit to the creative ideas for topics. We build the topics around our experts, who are able and willing to lead the group. The groups are interactive; with the leader prepared to give a five minute talk to begin the group's conversation. The Job Seekers ask questions and offer discussion on issues or concerns they have experienced. The program is one hour long. The Job Seekers change roundtable choices three times thus allowing them to sit in on three 18-minute discussions. This program, by far, is one of our most popular programs and generates our largest attendance. Our resume review team and workshop leaders enjoy the interaction as well. They all go home really tired after a full evening of participating in the dinner, resume review, then giving of their knowledge and time as Roundtable Leaders. We offer this program four times a year!

We build the topics around our experts, who are able and willing to lead the group.

Our Panel of Experts program consists of three professionals and a moderator. Usually the panel is made up of one Executive Search Firm Recruiter, a Contract Recruiter, and Human Resources Hiring Manager. We have varied the mix of expertise but this combination seems to cover all the questions and issues Job Seekers encounter daily in their searches. To control the types of questions asked, the moderator will often come prepared with 20 questions which she/he gives to the panel and also "plants" in the audience by giving the questions in advance to 20 different Job Seekers to ask. There are no lulls in the flow of the questions and answers, since the questions are already out in the audience before the program begins. Often we have asked for questions to be put in a basket as well from the audience and passed forward to the moderator who then screens the questions in advance to prevent inappropriate or duplicate questions. This program comes together easily as we utilize our own resume review team and workshop leaders as well. Our most difficult part of the evening is stopping the questions and ending by 9:00 p.m.! We offer this program three times a year.

Speed Networking allows for the Job Seeker to practice networking and verbalizing their "30 Second Elevator Speech." It is not easy! The Job Seekers always walk away saying they had no idea how much work they needed to put into polishing up their presentation skills. What a great time to notice this! Nothing to lose here! Practice! Practice! Practice! During this one hour of interaction, the Job Seekers will repeat their "Speech" at least 10 times, listen to at least 20 others give their "speech," and exchange at least 25 cards! All walk away feeling they had "time well spent" and confident, or recognizing the need for additional work to go forward with their skills! Fantastic! We offer this program three or four times a year.

Since we meet on the second and fourth Monday of each month and considering several holiday conflicts, we end up having about 21-22 meetings per year. We have discussed a number of different meeting formats where our own volunteers define the program for about 8-10 of these meetings. For the remainder of the meetings, we will recruit industry experts to provide keynote addresses on specific areas of interest to our Job Seekers, as we discussed earlier. We have found this mix of speakers and programs to be most effective and attractive to our Job Seekers. We have found this to be a great balance!

Would You Like to Deliver a Keynote Address?

❖ ***Ruthie Powell Page 162***

CHAPTER 9

"Love the Lord your God with all your heart and with all your soul and with all your mind and with all your strength. The second is this: Love your Neighbor as yourself. There is no commandment greater than these."

Mark 12: 30-31

Can I Teach a Small Group Workshop?

Our program has workshops starting at 1:30 p.m., running prior to the main program and then again at a separate 45 minute period reserved for all interactive sessions. When we meet with church leaders during our one-to-one time, we stress how important it is to work with the gifts and talents God avails to us with each volunteer.

Workshops were the last piece of the Job Networking Ministry puzzle. The Speakers provided motivation and technical support in areas of interest. The dinners were bringing in a valuable spiritual component and caring support. The one-to-one resume reviews were giving Job Seekers a personal touch point with expert guidance in a very uncomfortable but critical area. Industry Guides were providing continued support for Job Seekers after they left the meeting. Now industry specific experts were asking if they could teach workshops.

The first workshop was Tim Morrison's class on "How to Write a Resume." Tim had been providing one-to-one resume review since resume review began. One night he said, "I've been thinking about resume review. Many of the mistakes made are rather common and repeated. I could cover most of the content in a small group workshop. The Job Seeker could then go back and make the corrections. The next time they would be ready for a polished conversation with one of our resume reviewers." What a great idea! We now had our first workshop.

Later, a professional Career Coach suggested that he would like to develop a 45 minute workshop to prepare Job Seekers for the interview process. He prepares material that he uses to begin discussion and provoke thinking and then opens the room to questions and answers. There is always the question about how and when to discuss salary, negotiations for pay, and how to answer difficult interview questions especially related to termination. The room is always full and interactive.

Another 45 minute workshop was developed by a man who starts by asking the question "Do you want to start your own business?" The workshop provokes thinking about the start up process as well as ownership joys and sorrows. Purchase of franchise opportunities are explored as well as training and costs.

An afternoon workshop was offered by husband and wife team who had been serving as resume reviewers. Together they own an executive search firm. He was a human resources director for over 20 years prior to starting their own practice in search. This workshop combines much of the basic preparation skills necessary to a Job Seeker to get started. He and his wife share the basics with the group beginning with developing a search plan, applying for positions, practicing for the interview, and role playing. Another portion of this afternoon workshop teaches how to handle finances during this time including the use of 401k and IRA money. All of these workshops were offered as volunteers saw their knowledge and gifts coming together with a purpose and a place that would allow them to share their gifts.

We had many requests during the workshop time to offer a way for Job Seekers to meet other Job Seekers from the same industry. So during the workshop time, we also created a small group setting where individuals could network by industry. We added signs to our dinner tables so they could become industry focused after dinner. Each table was now identified by industry, so that during our next time period Job Seekers could connect with each other in small industry focused groups. Through experimentation, we discovered about 20 different categories of industries that were most frequently requested and designated tables with appropriate signs to indicate gatherings. This is one of our most popular ways Job Seekers now spend the 45 minutes between the dinner and the keynote. Again, this program is simple to organize and practical for our Job Seekers.

The 45 minutes between the end of the dinner at 7:00 p.m. and the Keynote Speaker has become a rich opportunity for Job Seekers to choose between resume review, industry guides, and small group networking by industry and 45 minute workshops.

We then added a most important offering to the choices at this time! We asked our Prayer Ministry Leader to pull together a team of people who would be willing to come to the program for 45 minutes to pray with Job Seekers. We asked our Stephen's Ministers and others who like to pray to be available for prayer for our Job Seekers in our chapel. One Monday night, one of our Job Seekers leaving the chapel walked directly up to me, anxious to share what he had just experienced. He said with a deep look of peace on his face that, "I could go home right now! I really don't need anything more than I just had. I want you to know that an angel just prayed with me in the chapel and I feel so at peace. I just know everything is in God's hands and all this will turn out OK."

An angel just prayed with me in the chapel and I feel so at peace.

A full range of experiences are available during this 45 minute "break." One night we offered a Sanctuary Tour led by our senior pastor. Twenty-five people followed him to the sanctuary where he told them about the stained glass windows, brought them to the altar, prayed with them as a group, then one-to-one. Our pastor said it was one of the most powerful moments he had had in a long time. People of all faiths and no faith were reaching out for help and direction. This is a demonstration of the church being alive and meeting the needs in the lives of people today.

Learn more about how these workshops come together and operate by reading the stories from the leaders. Dr. Tim Morrison is a retired pastor, who today truly concentrates his time working with Job Seekers. He brings style and humor to a workshop focused on writing resumes that get results. Richard Kirby tells his story, taken from his experiences as a career coach. With a background that has taken him from Engineering, through Human Resources to Sales, he has some amazing insight for helping the Job Seeker. Bill Williams's engaging story takes him from an Army Officer to his current business helping individuals find their niche in the workplace.

Can I Teach a Small Group Workshop?

- ***Richard Kirby*** — ***Page 167***
- ***Bill Williams*** — ***Page 173***
- ***Tim Morrison*** — ***Page 177***

CHAPTER 10

"Love the Lord your God with all your heart and with all your soul and with all your mind. . . .
Love your neighbor as yourself."
Mark 22: 37-39

In Conclusion

You have now been introduced to the motivations behind, the development history and the mechanics of the program we call Job Networking. More importantly, you have heard directly from the people who participate and serve in this work. You have heard their stories, filled with passion, about the hearts of service and the miraculous ways lives have been changed through their service and faith.

Miracles happen and all are rewarded when giving people respond to a need by "loving their neighbor", simply by applying just a small piece of themselves where they are gifted and as they come together in community to serve. We hope that this book will help you feel better prepared and encouraged to simply "jump in" to help your "unemployed neighbors" in these uncertain times.

As you prepare yourselves or your faith community for building or expanding a Job Networking or career focused effort, we encourage you to consider the perspective and challenge as well as the lessons learned by Jay Litton, who has energized and directed this RUMC effort to love our neighbors through the RUMC Job Networking Ministry.

A Personal Perspective and Challenge

Imagine using your unique God given gifts to serve others in need for Him. There are probably thousands of ways to make this happen. However the one ministry that has had the most impact on me has been the Job Networking Ministry.

My family moved to Roswell, Georgia, in 1994 with our three small children after my office was eliminated due to a downsizing in Cincinnati, Ohio. We decided to call Roswell our home to put us back in the South. Although I was raised in the church I stopped attending after I went to college like many other people. My wife and I attended various churches during our marriage but I did not consider myself a believer. My wife wanted us to attend church regularly for the kids so I went along for that reason. After checking out a few churches in the community we became regular visitors at Roswell United Methodist Church.

In early 1997 I was aware that my income was 50% less than the previous years before we moved to Roswell. I was in technology sales but I had chosen to work for an employee-owned company that had a great work environment but just did not pay well. I decided I needed to make a change.

In preparing for a job interview a few weeks later I made the decision to be "over prepared" in order to differentiate myself from the other candidates that they'd be interviewing. I decided to conduct the interview in a similar way I would sell to potential clients – I put in writing specific ideas on how I could contribute to the company if I was hired. It took some risk because I didn't know everything about the job or company but I felt like I had nothing to lose. It worked so well that I received job offers from both companies accepting what I thought was the better offer.

Later that summer I read Steven Covey's book The *Seven Habits of Successful People*. The book made me realize that I was not involved in volunteer work. I was just taking care of the family and working at my job.

A few months later our Minister dedicated one sermon to volunteering. I felt a need to get involved. We were handed a pamphlet describing over 125 volunteer opportunities at the church and the one that stood out to me was Job Networking. I wasn't in Human Resources or Recruiting but I began thinking that maybe I could help people with my interview strategy ideas.

At our meetings we would have about 10-15 Job Seekers show up and we would point them to community resources and discuss their needs.

Big things can happen when people serve Him.

About two years later my wife and children wanted to join the church. The Sunday was selected but I wasn't ready. After all, don't you have to give your life to Christ when you join a church?

My heart was softening though. Over the previous years a few people engaged with me in conversations about why I was not a Christian. They were persuasive but I continued to challenge God. Even a Christian upbringing was not enough for me. When that Sunday arrived I sat in the pew knowing that I had to make a decision. Was I going to join my family in front of the church or just stay seated? I decided to pray while in the pew and ask God to come into my heart and take charge of my life. Later that day I let my wife know of my decision and my outlook on life has never been the same.

After a couple years at Job Networking I was the only volunteer left after my volunteer partner Debbie Reid had an extended illness. At one meeting shortly after she left I had only one Job Seeker show up. Although it was just the two of us, I felt that if I was helping just one person then that worked for me. I learned through that experience that Job Networking can happen for any church with just one volunteer and one Job Seeker and no budget.

After a few more months, I realized that we were offering a great service at our church, but something was missing. We were not inviting God into our Job Networking meetings. That had to change. We needed to change this from a program to a ministry.

I began to include prayer to our meetings which doesn't sound like much but we had not done that before. I then tried to recruit volunteers to add new ideas and energy. More importantly, these new volunteers allowed God to work through them. We then asked the Job Seekers to include God in their job search. Everything seemed to start to come together.

Today we have many dozens of volunteers that are very passionate about serving and being a witness for Christ. Big things can happen when people serve Him.

Some things I have learned the past dozen years in running our meetings at RUMC:

- Make God #1 in your meetings for both your volunteers and Job Seekers;
- Create your ministry so it is Lay led instead of being led by a Pastor or staff member;
- Grow your ministry by letting your volunteers contribute in areas of the ministry that they feel are right for them;
- Look for leadership opportunities for your volunteers;
- Find ways to bring in dozens of volunteers without having them attend organizational meetings (eg. Industry Guide Program);
- Network in your community constantly by asking as many people as possible, "Do you know anyone looking for work?" If they do, ask, "Are you helping them network?"

When they say no, tell them about your next meeting. It works and you have an opportunity to witness about your faith-based meetings if you so choose;

- Give your Job Seekers personal attention when they walk in the door to your meetings. A warm greeting kicks off their experience in the right way;
- Help other churches start their own ministry. This isn't about my church but about multiplying our efforts together for Him.

We have a great opportunity to serve people that are in need. God is always trying to get our attention and a career transition may be one of the greatest opportunities we have to point people to Him.

Jay Litton:

I've been volunteering at RUMC Job Networking since 1997 and work as the Regional Sales Manager for Guardian Edge. With 29 years of sales/sales management experience, I try to leverage my experiences to help those in transition. I'm also the creator of the Wow! Interview™ and have taught over 10,000 people this system on how to get the offer they want. I've been married for 27 years and have three children and one daughter in law.

CHAPTER 11

Stories from the Volunteers

Dan's Story

Tagged to Start a New Ministry to the Job Seekers

I will admit that God had been calling me to start a career ministry at my church (First Baptist Church Woodstock) for years. But like many, I felt I was under qualified, not worthy or simply made excuses for not having enough time in my life. Let's face it; I was already actively involved in other associations and networking groups. How could I find time to start something like a career ministry? I was an active member, a board member and past president of the Institute of Management Accountants (IMA), an organization of over 700 accountants in Atlanta. I've served in my Sunday school class as Care Group Leader and teacher. For years, I've coached and continue to coach my son's baseball teams. I'm involved in High Tech Ministry and an ongoing Grace@Work Bible study. The truth is I was not willing to allow myself enough time with God so He could clear my calendar and let me do His will.

Like many, I focused on improving my work life but did not devote enough time on my spiritual life. I spent a lot of energy on the "financial security" that my job brings and worked over time both night and day "branding" my experience and expertise. Part of that branding evolved into speaking to area associations on employment trends and hiring practices. Through various connections, I had an opportunity to speak at Georgia Association of Personnel Services (GAPS) in November of 2008.

The association was made up of mostly industry recruiters and hiring managers in and around Atlanta. After my presentation, several people came up and introduced themselves. To my good fortune, one of them was Katherine Simons. She shared how she was involved with GAPS but more importantly, she began to tell me about Roswell United Methodist Church and its Job Networking Ministry. She said that she and others volunteered there several times a month and that they were always looking for potential speakers. She believed that what I had just shared would be interesting to present at one of their meetings. She connected me with Jay Litton and after several conversations I was scheduled to speak at their first meeting in January 2009.

The night of my speaking engagement at RUMC, I arrived early to set up the PowerPoint presentation. I was amazed at how organized all the volunteers were. Volunteers were arranging chairs, organizing name tags, positioning hand-outs in binders. Greeters were at the entrances greeting attendees and directing them to the right places. I spent nine years in the military. The military is organized. What I witnessed that evening was a well organized ministry. Everybody had their role. The job was getting done.

Shortly after the dinner and the timely spiritual message, the attendees began filing in. Hundreds of out of work people entered the auditorium. I noticed immediately there were all levels of people: from laborers to CEOs, executives, CFOs, human resources managers, accountants, administrative assistants, construction workers…all levels of experience and skills sets. A quick glance at the gathering clearly conveyed that the economic downturn had not just hit the unskilled, the transient or the homeless. The recession was unfortunately affecting all of America's working class, who were not experienced or equipped to handle it. We have not seen this level of unemployment before. Their resumes were not up-to-date. They didn't know how to differentiate themselves among the hundreds of thousands of unemployed workers. They didn't know what the Web 2.0 Revolution was or how social networking had become an integral part of our new society.

It seemed odd then how timely my message was; "What is your plan B?" I had been promoting that message for years through my work as an executive recruiter. I told everyone I met that you should always have a "what if plan." Now more than ever it was vital for the unemployed to develop such a plan.

I know that God placed me at the GAPS meeting and that our meeting was not by chance. God connected us as He always does. God works delightfully in and out of our lives and when we ignore His will, He always finds a path for us to rejoin Him in His work.

I spent nine years in the military. The military is organized. What I witnessed that evening was a well organized ministry.

Throughout the evening, I continued to meet volunteers who were out of work and I was blessed by their faithful hearts to serve. Even though they were unemployed, they felt there was work to be done. There's always work in God's company and if you are unemployed God is always hiring. I once read that God doesn't pay very much, but the benefits are out of this world.

My heart was inspired that night at RUMC to help God's people and to share my knowledge and experience in the job search process. Before leaving that night I asked if I could come back to volunteer during their meetings. If I was going to be faithful and start a career ministry in my home base, one of Atlanta's largest churches, I would need all the training and support that they could provide.

The bottom line is that you only need three things to start a career ministry:

- Lots of prayer;
- A faithful heart to respond to God and let other's know;
- A willingness to act.

God has already put the plan in motion and has already redirected volunteers with hearts to serve. It's that simple!

The creation of Cornerstone Career Ministry at First Baptist Church Woodstock was all God's work. The following Sunday after speaking at RUMC, I was sitting in Sunday school talking to a good friend and now co-founder of Cornerstone Career Ministry, Steve Allen. Apparently, God had been working on his heart to serve as a career advisor in the job search process. Steve had years of experience in financial management for large and midsize organizations. He had hired (and fired) many and was himself in the job search process for the third time in his life. He knew the ropes from both sides of the employment game and better yet, he had a heart to serve. He outlined his vision and I outlined mine. Our thoughts were amazingly identical.

We met for breakfast and spoke at church and drew out plans for the ministry. Based on our discussions, we felt we needed eight areas of responsibility and a Committee Chair to lead each area of the ministry.

- Prayer/Counseling;
- Greeting/Volunteer;
- Program/Speakers;
- Industry Guides;
- Communications;
- Funding/Sponsor;
- Technical Support;
- Food Services/Facility

We wanted and needed the church involved and we needed to make sure that the Jobs Ministry at First Baptist Church and the director Bill Plymale were on board. Again, it is amazing how God plants the seeds. For months, Bill had been praying to God to send him volunteers who would be able to help with outreach within the community on job searching. We presented the ministry outline to the church and within the next week there was an announcement in the church bulletin. People quickly responded as they called to volunteer - each with the unique skills and passion that we needed. For the next several months, Steve and I attended and volunteered at RUMC as Table Hosts, Resume Reviewers and Industry Guides. We borrowed everything we could, asked many questions and left with a number of forms. It was all given willingly.

In March of 2009, Cornerstone Career Ministry was formed after months of planning. God had sent us all the required people with all the right spiritual skills just when we needed it. It is now very clear that if you seek God's grace and direction, you will find that He has already put the pieces in place. The ministry awaits you. You just need to pray, tell and do."

This March, Cornerstone Career Ministry celebrates its first year as a ministry. God has given us over 30 faithful volunteers each of whom has the heart to serve. We are blessed to have over 100 attendees every 1st and 3rd Tuesday of the month and although we first believed it to be impossible to carve out time from our busy schedules, God led us to find the time. We are truly amazed how blessed we are by those we serve, by those who come and by those who have taught us so much about giving. God has provided and He equips the called. *"But to each one of us grace has been given as Christ apportioned it." Ephesians 4:7*

Dan Guelzo:

I hold the title of National Practice Director Talent Strategy at Spherion and I am Co-Founder of Cornerstone Career Ministry. My email address is danielguelzo@spherion.com. I served nine years as a Tactical Air Control Officer in the United States Navy prior to entering recruiting within the Accounting/Finance, Banking, and Information Technology communities. My wife, Ginny, and our two children Katie and Austin live in East Cobb and attend First Baptist Church Woodstock, where I also teach Sunday school.

Reed's Story

Churches Learning From Each Other

My story is perhaps going to be different from others in the way I was called to serve in career ministry. In the fall of 2008, I received a telephone call from one of the associate pastors at Peachtree Road United Methodist Church asking me to join with a group of other individuals to develop Crossroads Career Ministry at our church. When I received this call I was anticipating that my work with Right Management as a career management consultant would conflict with my ability to attend the planning sessions and the sessions for Job Seekers, so I declined to participate at that time. In the spring of 2009, I began to rethink this request and decided to contact the associate pastor who had called me. I told her that I would begin to participate on the leadership team and start to attend the meetings. It became apparent to me that the group was going to need strong leadership in order to establish a successful job ministry program. At Right Management, I work with individuals, one-to-one and in groups to coach and teach job search skills.

I enjoy my work and get a great deal of personal and professional satisfaction out of helping others at a particularly difficult time in their lives. I had taken on a number of pro bono clients to assist them with their search, utilizing the knowledge and skills that I was acquiring as a result of my work. Since I was doing this work primarily for friends and family, I was not really considering it to be "volunteering" but just something that naturally evolved. In a questionnaire that I was asked to complete as part of our employment process, one of the questions asked was why I was interested in becoming a career management consultant. I answered this question with a response that I had a genuine and sincere desire to help other people who found themselves in career transition. I worked in human resources for over 30 years as a chief human resource officer with over 10 years in retail and 20 in large health care systems located across the country. During the time I worked in these health care systems, I recommended and began to utilize a number of different "outplacement" firms, now known as "career continuation" firms. My motivation to be involved in job ministry programs sprang from my positive experiences working with these firms helping people transition from one position to another.

Another strong motivator is based on the fact that I had personally experienced what it was like to lose a job and find another position. Given my relationship with the principals in these firms I was fortunate to have their counsel and support during my job transitions. This support was provided informally when it was my decision to seek a new position and also provided by my previous employer when we mutually concluded that it was time for me to leave. Some of these transitions took a fairly short period of time and others took considerably longer.

I wanted to share this background information with you, the reader, because it is the reason I was drawn to become a volunteer at Peachtree Road United Methodist Church. It seemed to come at a good time at the church as we were finishing our spring sessions and deciding if we wanted to continue this ministry in the fall. Some of these reservations revolved around having a fairly small number of people attending and the lack of having someone on the leadership team who had the experience and the desire not only to continue what we had started but to strengthen the program as well. With the support of the other members of the leadership team I quickly stepped into the role of a "servant leader."

Working in the position of career management consultant, I was very much aware of the need to help our candidates get involved with at least one job networking group in the Atlanta metropolitan area. When I was working in one of our career centers I asked if we had a list of these networking groups that we could provide to our candidates. After determining that no such list existed, the center manager requested that I develop this list so we could make it available to our candidates. As I began to research these groups, I heard very favorable comments about the career ministry at Roswell United Methodist Church. I thought about what we might do differently at Peachtree United Methodist Church. I decided to arrange a visit to RUMC in the afternoon before one of their meetings along with two other members of our leadership team. They were very generous with their time. They outlined the history of their program and how it evolved over the years to be the program that is offered today.

These volunteer programs also provide for emotional and spiritual support so people can realize they are not alone in this journey.

At the conclusion of our time together, I was asked if I would be willing to serve as a Table Host that evening. Since this was my first visit to Roswell, I was somewhat reluctant, but I was persuaded that I could quickly assimilate this role. I had such a positive experience serving as a Table Host and participating in the evening program that the next day I joined the RUMC ministry team both as a Table Host and resume reviewer. I felt that the Lord was calling me to utilize my skills and knowledge along with the compassion that I have for people who are in career transition. I decided to volunteer my time at Roswell and strengthen the ministry at Peachtree Road.

I believe that one of the reasons I have been successful in my current position is based on the fact that I can relate to the concerns and feelings that people have when they lose a job and need to find another. I have experienced this same process myself. This experience has helped me set aside the time to volunteer in two career ministry programs. This first-hand experience has also made it easier for me to recommend to my client candidates and my pro bono candidates to attend one or both of these programs or to find one in an area that might be closer to their home. These groups provide practical knowledge through their speakers that individuals can use in their job search. In addition, these volunteer programs also provide for emotional and spiritual support so people can realize they are not alone in this journey. They now have the support of people they meet at these sessions and are reminded to rely on their relationship with God.

Given the high unemployment rate in the Atlanta metropolitan area, individuals from many different industries and professions have lost their positions. There is a great deal of competition for positions, on average six candidates for every available position. Teaching current and contemporary job search skills and reinforcing the power of networking, both personal and virtual through such sites as LinkedIn, will accelerate the candidate's job search. Finding ways to "network" their way into a company rather than relying on the traditional cover letter and resume will bring much better results. Career ministry helps individuals acquire the knowledge and skills needed to successfully navigate the current job market. Job ministries that are available to individuals in Atlanta help build their personal networks, which is the most crucial aspect in conducting a successful search. My experience is that approximately eight or nine out of ten people will find their next job through networking.

For churches that are considering this type of job ministry, I can assure you that the need is there. Establishing a program will be beneficial not only to the church's own membership but to other individuals in the community who are seeking knowledge and support as they embark on a search for a new position. Many Job Seekers begin after lengthy periods of steady employment and need all the assistance that can be provided to plan a search process. Churches that have embarked on this ministry are heeding the call for a ministry that will support the needs of the next decade. They are fulfilling a real need as they respond to individuals at one of the most difficult times of their lives.

I want to conclude by briefly outlining the new program agenda for the Peachtree Road United Methodist Church Job Seeker ministry:

6:30 p.m. to 6:45 p.m. Greeting and Welcome

- This is meant to allow those who attend to visit with each other and the leadership team. We also include an opening reflection.

6:45 p.m. to 7:45 p.m. Speaker

- Guest Speaker who delivers a message that is relevant and useful to the Job Seekers.

7:45 p.m. to 8:45 p.m. Roundtable Discussions

- These discussions enable the participants to interact with the speaker and one another to discuss any particular success or issues that they have encountered in their search.

8:45 p.m. Closing

- Closing Reflection and Invitation to attend our next session.

At the close of our meeting one of our members reviews the sign-in list reflecting the type of position being sought and matches it with an Industry Guide. The Industry Guide gives 15-20 minutes of time on the telephone or using email to help individuals with their search and to build their personal network. In addition, I send out an email to everyone who has attended that contains a spiritual message and our contact information to encourage further networking.

Reed A. Harvey:

I am the servant leader for Peachtree Road United Methodist Church Career Transition Support Group and I volunteer at Roswell United Methodist Church as a Table Host and resume reviewer. For nearly the last four years I have worked as a career management consultant for Right Management in Atlanta. I have been married for 44 years and have two children, one of whom resides in Atlanta and the other in New York City.

I can be reached at reedaharvey@yahoo.com.

Chris' Story

From Job Seeker to Volunteer

My first experience with RUMC was as a Job Seeker. I was very familiar with the reputation of RUMC's Job Networking Ministry. With a background in Human Resources and many years of consulting, I had become a Stephen Minister several years earlier, and volunteered at Mt. Bethel UMC's Jobs Ministry for over four years. My spiritual activities had provided a new energy and direction. I loved connecting with people in transition and was amazed at the stories of their own personal and professional transformations. By design, Mt. Bethel's Jobs Ministry met on the first and third Monday nights to complement RUMC's ministry which meets on the second and fourth Monday evenings.

In 2006, I began a new chapter in my life. As a "newly single" person, I had moved from East Cobb to Roswell, and joined Northbrook UMC. Part of my journey includes the exploration of a different work focus, so I decided to visit RUMC's Job Networking Ministry. I persuaded a friend to go with me. As we approached the entrance, the doors flung open, and we were greeted by two smiling men who welcomed us with personal warmth and attention. I have no doubt that God was present that evening. A volunteer whom I had met at Mt. Bethel's Jobs Ministry introduced me to RUMC and encouraged me to volunteer.

The program that evening happened to be Roundtables, which offered multiple topics and speakers, of which we could choose three. I was amazed and impressed by the information and expertise that was so generously shared. At that point, I had no way of knowing that I would soon be a regular presenter of one of these Roundtable sessions. And so it began…I was hooked!

I returned to RUMC in two weeks as a volunteer resume reviewer, and it was great! My commitment to volunteer meant "no excuses" for not returning on a regular basis. Not only was I able to provide one-to-one resume feedback, but I was also able to benefit from hearing the latest career advice from a variety of top-notch speakers. By the time the next Roundtable meeting was scheduled, I was asked to be a group leader. I had presented a program at Mt. Bethel on Behavioral Interviews, which would be an excellent addition to the list of topics. Next came an invitation to participate with the "Ask an Expert" panel, another regularly-scheduled program. OK, so the job search is serious, but that doesn't mean we have to be solemn in how we share our expertise! My latent desire to be a stand-up comic unsuspectingly emerged that night. Of course, I can't recall the stories I told, but I do remember that Jay had stepped out of the room and heard laughter erupt at several intervals. Evidently he returned to see what was going on inside. I imagine most of the stories were embarrassing things I had said or done over the years. I also realized – once again – the therapeutic value of humor and laughter.

By this time, I had the second and fourth Monday evenings anchored solidly on my schedule each month. I really looked forward to the meetings. The warmth and enthusiasm of all the volunteers never wavered – they had become a "faith family" filled with uplifting care and support. It was wonderful to see so many other Job Seekers attend regularly, and to see how they opened up to the genuine and tangible assistance this ministry provided for them.

I still leave each meeting knowing that this ministry has been a blessing for so many people who may be feeling hurt, frightened and desperate. Yes, the volunteers all have experience in a variety of areas; however, I believe our greatest contribution is the compassion, hope and encouragement we convey to the Job Seekers. God works through each of us when we talk with someone who feels hopeless. Often, I don't know whom God has touched through me. But there is no greater "high" than talking to someone who has hit rock-bottom, and then experiences a "heart transformation." I know it is God who plants the seeds of hope and joy in our words and actions. We demonstrate God's love by sharing our own genuine care and concern. This is the core of the ministry.

When the "Developing Your Spiritual Resume" dinners were added to the schedule, I was asked to be a Table Host. We had no way of knowing how these dinners would significantly change our Monday nights. From the very first dinner, I felt this was the primary method for us to touch people's hearts, hear their worries, and uplift them by "walking God's talk." Prior to the dinners, attendance had grown so large, that it was very easy for someone to blend into the crowd, sit in the back row, and not really participate in the meetings. Now, sitting at a table with eight other Job Seekers and a Table Host, it became nearly impossible to disengage as a bystander. I recall how one man revealed that he had tried for many months to attend one of the Job Networking meetings at RUMC. He said he would arrive at the church, but just could not get out of the car. That provided such insight on how vulnerable and uneasy some Job Seekers feel when they are in transition. I watched friendships evolve during dinner and the table discussion, which followed the speaker. I've had Job Seekers pull me aside after dinner, and express concern about another person at the table who seemed particularly despondent or depressed. I've witnessed weary, experienced Job Seekers guide others who were just embarking on their searches. I've hugged, cried and prayed with countless individuals who felt safe in sharing their deepest concerns.

As my volunteer roles expanded in this ministry, the Reverend Melinda Jones, Associate Pastor for Congregational Care at the church I attend, asked me to brainstorm with her on how we could provide resources and guidance for our members. She saw a void and need for career assistance at Northbrook UMC, just a few miles away. She knew so many families whose work and income had been impacted by the soft economy. We explored how we could provide resources and guidance for our church family. We talked at length about all the services and tools that were solidly in place at RUMC – there was certainly no need to duplicate programs or efforts. We determined we could encourage our members to take advantage of RUMC's offerings and also provide supplemental programs that were more personalized in scope. This approach aligned with our church's "personality," since our congregation is active in many missions, and very friendly. And so Northbrook UMC's Career Ministry was born!

One man....had tried for many months to attend...but just could not get out of the car.

Northbrook's church leadership agreed that we should become a part of the Crossroads Career Network. We also determined that we would offer the six-part workshop, "Maximizing Your Career in Turbulent Times," along with the online career assessment available through Crossroads Career Network. I was very familiar with current professional career materials, and knew all the content was outstanding! What an amazing gift to have all the key aspects of a job search already compiled and packaged beautifully – and the Bible passages included were absolutely perfect. Since I am an experienced facilitator, I agreed to teach the sessions. We advertised the workshops in our church, and also within the RUMC communication channels. Brian and Kristy Ray were incredibly supportive and helpful in offering suggestions (including contact names) for how the workshops could be presented. To date, we've held the workshop twice. The first session was led on two Saturday mornings, and we had just about an even mix of members and non-members who attended. Our overall reaction was that the workshop was too rushed for the necessary content to be covered. With that in mind, our second workshop was offered on eight consecutive Wednesday nights. This was one of several classes held after Wednesday Night Supper, with childcare arrangements already in place. The schedule was more relaxed. We had much more time for rich discussion. Coincidentally, I met Greg Losh through our volunteer work at RUMC. It turns out Greg is a Human Resources professional, and a member of Northbrook! Greg and I co-led the second workshop, which provided a great balance of perspective and styles. We intend to offer several workshops throughout the year. Melinda and I continue to explore how we can expand this important ministry.

While my roles and passion for career ministry expanded, I recognized a transformation within myself. I examined and adjusted my values and priorities, significantly deepened my faith, and continually learned from listening to and guiding others in their career searches. As I became more involved with the lives of people in job transition, I discovered my true passion and professional direction. My consulting practice is now focused on career coaching. I also contract with the world's largest talent and career management consulting firm. After many years in the workplace, I believe I've found my "calling." I'm so grateful that I was called down so many paths that led exactly to where I am today.

***Chris Gilliam*:**

I am a volunteer with the RUMC Job Networking Ministry, and have served in many roles, including dinner speaker. I'm very active at Northbrook UMC, and began our Career Ministry there. My career began in HR at The Coca-Cola Company; since then I've been a Coach and HR Consultant based in Marietta, Birmingham, Nashville, Baltimore, and the Middle Eastern country of Bahrain. Additionally, I work for Right Management as a Career Management Consultant. My children are very responsible (and funny) young adults, and a joy to be near! The best email address for contacting me is chris.gilliam@comcast.net.

Curt's Story

The Mt. Bethel U.M.C. Career Ministry Story

Mt. Bethel United Methodist Church is an 8,000 member church located in Marietta, Georgia. Mt. Bethel had an active "Jobs Ministry" in the early 2000's. The program was eventually discontinued in 2006 as the relatively informal format of the ministry seemed to lose its effectiveness and the economy improved to a point where there was not as much of a demand for the service. During the last year of the ministry, I visited the RUMC Job Networking Ministry to observe the ministry's format and determine if there were opportunities to duplicate any of the ministry components at Mt. Bethel.

While the Mt. Bethel ministry was eventually discontinued, I was so impressed with the format and effectiveness of this ministry that I became a volunteer conducting resume reviews, participating in the roundtable presentations, and eventually becoming a Table Host for the dinners. Over a two year period, I had an opportunity to observe and be involved in all aspects of their ministry and in the fall of 2008, was invited by the leaders to attend a Crossroads Career Network training session in Atlanta. What I hadn't realized was that God had intervened and was preparing me for a request from Mt. Bethel's senior pastor, Randy Mickler. In November of 2008, I was asked to re-introduce the Jobs Ministry as the economy had worsened significantly and many Mt. Bethel members were out of work.

I contacted several of the previous Mt. Bethel Jobs Ministry volunteers and we met with the church administrator and Director of Volunteers in December of 2008 to plan the ministry. We set a goal of having our first meeting in February of 2009. Our first order of business was to agree to join the Crossroads Career Network. That would provide us with the guidance and resources to jumpstart our ministry. As we went through the planning process there was much discussion with regard to the format of the ministry. I was well prepared for that discussion, based upon my experience as a volunteer at RUMC, the information that I gained from the Crossroads Career training session, and resources that were made available to us through our membership in the Crossroads Career Network.

In thinking through our ministry format, we decided that we would focus on preparing Job Seekers with the basic tools to launch a job search through several content-focused presentations. Rather than trying to duplicate the more networking-focused formats that are used at RUMC and many other ministries, we would develop an approach which would be complementary to that format. For example, rather than using different outside speakers, we elected to develop three presentations which are continually rotated, so each presentation is given once every three meetings. The three presentations are: “Developing Your Personal Brand and Marketing Materials,” “Leveraging Technology in Your Job Search,” and "Interviewing for Success and Negotiating Your Compensation Package.” Each of the sessions is designed to be approximately 90 minutes in length and is delivered with a PowerPoint presentation which includes handouts of the presentation and other materials such as a list of interview questions and a packet of resume examples. The three sessions are designed to be "hands on" and interactive. Our attendance generally varies from 15 to 25 attendees so the group is small enough to support questions and interactive discussions.

On months that have a 5th Tuesday, we have offered other content-focused programs including such subjects as finding a job in the not-for-profit sector and marketing yourself as a contractor. The “5th Tuesday” programs provide some flexibility to vary our content while still focusing on the “job search basics” strategy.

In addition to the main presentation, we begin our meeting with a one-hour session in which volunteers review resumes and provide coaching for Job Seekers. The resume review and coaching are provided from 6:30 p.m. to 7:30 p.m. and the main presentation begins at 7:30 p.m. and continues until 9:00 p.m. We meet on the second and fourth Tuesday of every month. We made a conscious decision to conduct our meetings at times which were complementary to the other ministries in the area, as opposed to trying to compete with them.

We elected to develop three presentations which are continually rotated.

Mt. Bethel Career Ministry's niche is "job search preparation basics." We fully expect that Job Seekers will attend our ministry no more than three times, not including the "5th Tuesday" programs. At the end of each session we present the opportunities available through the Crossroads Career Website and the Crossroads Career Network of participating churches. We explain the format of some of the ministries which are provided by churches in the North Fulton and East Cobb County areas and provide a handout which lists many of the Crossroads Career Network churches in the immediate area. For example, we encourage Job Seekers to attend the Johnson Ferry Baptist Church six-week Career Explorer Program or Weekend Career Explorer Boot Camp. For Job networking, we encourage Job Seekers to attend the RUMC Job Networking Ministry and the North Point Community Church 3CG networking events.

As we have developed the Mt. Bethel Career Ministry, two of our biggest challenges have been obtaining volunteers and marketing our program. During the planning of the ministry, we advertised for volunteers in church publications and conducted several informational meetings so that potential volunteers could familiarize themselves with the ministry and volunteer opportunities. As with most volunteer opportunities, we began with a larger group of volunteers which, over the year, has been reduced in size to those who have more of a passion for the ministry. We designed the ministry format for flexibility with regard to volunteer involvement. Two volunteers are trained to conduct the three main sessions and there are approximately eight volunteers who participate in the resume reviews with at least three to four participating at any given meeting. We have an additional volunteer who handles the sign-in list and ensures that participants receive the appropriate handouts for each meeting.

As we began the ministry, we developed summaries of the three sessions which are included on a special Career Ministry section of the church's website. The week before each meeting the summary for the next session is publicized in the church bulletin and a church news e-mail blast to all members. As indicated above, each Career Ministry attendee is asked to sign a registration sheet which includes their e-mail address. We add each attendee to a database which receives an invitation to each of our meetings. Each Monday and Tuesday before our career ministry meeting the ministry is advertised on the church marquee. We have found that many of our attendees attend our meeting because of that advertisement.

As we develop our ministry, we have decided that we can be most effective by coordinating with the North Atlanta Crossroads Career Network of churches. Since we have chosen a focused niche for our ministry and with the services we offer, our attendees can best be served by encouraging them to expand their networking in other Crossroads churches, who offer different opportunities then we offer.

The Crossroads Career Network does an outstanding job of identifying different approaches and services for implementing a career ministry. The materials which are offered on the website provide the basis for a "turnkey" career ministry for any church.

The biggest challenge in starting a career ministry is to work through a process of identifying the ministry components that are best for your church environment. Brian and Kristy Ray are master career ministry consultants who provide guidance from their vast experience. If you are considering beginning a career ministry, I urge you to join the Crossroads Career Network, review the Crossroads Career materials, review your ideas with Brian and Kristy Ray, and then visit other Crossroads churches. The Crossroads Career Network has done the "heavy lifting." It's like buying a franchise. All you have to do is choose the programs and services and recruit volunteers.

Curt Engelmann:

I am a volunteer at the RUMC Job Networking Ministry and co-lead the Mt. Bethel UMC Career Ministry. My career has focused on human resources management, where I have served in both corporate and consulting executive roles. I am currently Managing Director of TALinsight, LLC, an Atlanta based human resources firm which specializes in compensation management and candidate screening systems.

I can be reached at cengelmann@talinsight.com .

John's Story

Looking Back Over the Years

As I look back over the past nine years of my involvement with the RUMC Job Networking Ministry, I rejoice at what God has done. He has led the growth and scope of this ministry. I believe strongly our growth has come as a direct result of God blessing this ministry.

In 2001, I had been retired a little over a year. We had joined RUMC and were members of a great Sunday School Class: The Seekers Class. We were encouraged to become involved in the actives of the church. I became interested in the Job Networking Ministry because I felt I could "bring something to the table" since my employment background involved the review of hundreds of resumes, and the interviewing and employment of many employees. I had worked directly with our Department of Human Resources. My employment of 37 years had me connected to the employment needs of Job Seekers. I was also directly involved with our sales force of over 1,300 sales reps. You might say that I was in the "people business" for a long time.

The memory of my first visit to a job networking meeting remains clear. We met in a small Sunday School Class room. There were approximately 15 Job Seekers present. The entire meeting was conducted by Jay Litton, our leader, and Neal Reynolds. I stood at the door to welcome and sign-in those attending. Oh yes, we served donuts which Neal had picked-up, but as I remember we did not have any coffee or cokes.

After a few months, our group grew larger so we moved into a much larger meeting room. It soon became apparent we needed more volunteers. During those early days I would bring home three to five resumes which I had been asked to review. I would review each one and email my recommendations to the applicant. This was a far cry from the professional resume reviewers we have today.

Each year our church would sponsor a Volunteer Fair. This was to introduce and explain the many ministries available at RUMC. One year the Fair was being held in our Fellowship Hall, and many of the ministries had tables set up and properly furnished with their material. We decided we had to do more to become noticed. We assembled a tent which we set-up in the middle of the Fellowship Hall. In addition, we had purchased some very colorful shirts for the volunteers to wear. We were the "hit" of the Fair, and we were able to recruit several new volunteers. We have continued our presence at the Volunteer Fairs.

Members of RUMC began taking notice of the RUMC Job Networking Ministry. When I first became a volunteer only a few members had any knowledge of our ministry.

Our Job Seekers continued to grow in number making it necessary to move again into a larger room. Then in a short period of time we moved into our Fellowship Hall which is our largest space for meetings. The RUMC Job Networking Ministry was really beginning to take roots, and had become a large and vital ministry.

It was somewhere during this period that a major decision was made. That decision involved God being more involved in our ministry. We closed our meetings with a prayer, but God had placed a call on Jay Litton to allow Him to become more visible in this ministry. I remember the conversation concerning this. We agreed we would open each meeting with prayer and close each meeting with prayer. Our ministry would also make it a central point to "Involve God in Your Job Search."

It was around this time we added the "Prayer Basket" for those requesting special prayers to place their request. Of the Job

Seekers attending our meetings very few were actually members of our church. Not everyone attending even had a faith. We did not want to drive away anyone, but the call to allow God into our ministry was too strong to reject. Let me add here that I do not think we lost anyone. Today, we still have non-Christians and those of Jewish traditions who attend our meetings.

Not too long after we had moved into the Fellowship Hall, we were asked to move our meetings to the gym in the "Dod." The Dod is the name given to the Youth Building at our church. The gym turned out to be the very best location we had ever had for our meetings. In fact, the location was perfect for us. God again had guided us to the best place for our meetings.

We would arrive early and place signs around our campus to direct Job Seekers to the Dod. We were now serving cokes, ice water, coffee and the famous chocolate chip cookies; baked and donated by Michael and Donna Dubois. The gym had a stage where we could showcase first class talent to present the programs. To this day, I do not know how we have been able to recruit these business leaders to present professional programs twice each month, twelve months a year.

By this time, the Industry Guide Program was in full swing and RUMC Job Networking had grown to an unbelievable level. We now had faithful volunteers to assist in all the activities. The resume review program had grown to where it now required three rooms for its activities.

After the initial set-up had been completed, I enjoyed being a Greeter. We placed two greeters at the double door entrance. As the Job Seeker arrived, both doors would swing open, and each person was greeted with a smile, a welcome, and a hand shake. Then, other greeters provided information and directions.

We had progressed with our sign-in procedure. One table was set up for first time visitors and a second table for repeat visitors. We collected the names, addresses, and email information from all attending.

Those who were repeat visitors only had to check their name rather than giving the information again. Everyone was asked to make a name tag, and we even explained why it was important to place the name tag on the right side.

With attendance reaching 250 Job Seekers, professional speakers delivering great programs, the resume review program growing each month, new seminars being added, volunteers growing in number and contribution AND with everything going so well – Why would we want to change anything?

The call to allow God into our ministry was too strong to reject.

Well, our next call was to feed the Job Seekers. Feed them with both food and spiritual growth. Why not begin our programs an hour earlier and have a meal along with a program of "Spiritual Growth?" God was about to become more involved than we had ever imaged.

At first, our ministry did not have a budget. We did not receive any direct financial assistance, but we did get the coffee donated. Of course, the church did provide the space, the room set-up and equipment, along with a supply of literature, books and Bibles. We certainly did not have the budget to provide a meal to hundreds of Job Seekers. But, our leadership had strong faith and they believed God would provide a way for this to happen. Somehow donations came in and the meals got off to a great start.

At first the Job Seekers would meet in the Fellowship Hall. While enjoying their meal they would have an hour of spiritual growth training and then walk across the campus back to the Dod for the balance of the meeting. I was blessed when I was asked to be the Greeter at the main door to the Fellowship Hall. What a joy to greet hundreds of people and to welcome them to our Job Networking Ministry. Before the Spiritual Session was completed, I would go back to the Dod and again greet and welcome the visitors.

It was not long before the number of Job Seekers grew so large we had to leave the Dod and consolidate all our meetings in the same building with the Fellowship Hall.

To look at our Job Networking Ministry today, one would say WOW! A building is constructed one brick at a time, and a Job Networking Ministry is much the same. As long as there are dedicated volunteers, talented leadership, and as long as God is involved and at the center of the ministry, it will succeed.

I have served on the Board of Stewards, and on many church committees. None of these has given me the satisfaction and the blessings received from Job networking. Several members of my family have been caught up in the recent "down-sizing" which has gripped America. I know the pain, the difficulty, the hurt, the embarrassment, and the problems caused by one losing his/her job. We are assisting men and women who were employed for 20-25 years, and due to no fault of their own, they find themselves unemployed. Most have not developed a resume nor developed interviewing skills. They need help.

It has been a blessing from heaven to try to help these people.

***John Harper*:**
I am a Volunteer at the RUMC Job Networking Ministry, and a member of RUMC since 2001. I retired from Zep Manufacturing Company in 1999, after 37 years of employment where I served as Vice President of Operations. At RUMC I have served as Vice Chair for the Board of Stewards, member of the "In His Steps "Gifts Steering Committee, and the Senior Adult Committee. I presently serve on the Pastor-Parish Relations Committee, President of the PrimeTime Singers and enjoy being a Greeter on Sunday mornings. I am blessed with a wonderful family with grandchildren and two great grandchildren.

Donna's Story

Job Networking and Me

I have been in the background volunteering for many years... supplying cokes, making copies by the 1000's, putting up signs or taking them down and running interference for Jay, but almost never going to the meetings.

When the last two of our three children left for college, I decided it would be nice to volunteer together with Jay. This is after I had been running the home front on Monday nights for 11 years, so he could volunteer at Job Networking. I was known in the youth department of the church and he was known in job networking area of the church and those two areas didn't mingle. I don't think we ever volunteered together unless it was a Sunday school project.

Just as the thought of volunteering crossed my mind, I was approached to help with the new dinner program that was being started before the main meeting. It was perfect for me. I like a small job that is not in the lime light. So the dinners and I started together and we have both grown. I started as a server, and then I came early to set up and now help oversee the table leaders. We try to make sure there is a table leader at each table of Job Seekers. We also have all the resources ready for them as they walk in the door. Their packet has prayer cards, the message cards from the dinner speaker, the handouts for the night and anything else they may need. Most of our work is done before the dinner begins. It is nice to be on a team where we all pitch in and get it done without a thought to asking who is in charge and who should be working on this.

Even though I help with career assessment testing and career tools with our small business, this is a different experience. At Job Networking, we help people not only with the practical tools they need for their job search and the networking avenue, we also help people are hurting and need someone to care, to give them a smile and a warm welcome. We give them all a little bit of love, a little bit of food and a little bit of hope to take home with them.

It is part of my "Martha" mentality to serve, fix, organize and mother. Helping with the dinner part of the Job Networking Ministry is a good fit for me.

It has been a great experience to be involved with such a giving and worthwhile ministry. I love how many ways there are for people to volunteer. There is an army of people required for setting up for 200-350 for dinner. This is a big change from the 80 folks we started serving at the beginning!! I really like that we use cloth table clothes and real silverware for the dinners. It helps the Job Seeker feel like it is a special dinner and not a cheap, quick dinner experience just to feed them. The greeters are so special. They give each Job Seeker a warm welcome as they enter and are led to a table. The dinner servers are always ready with a smile. The table leaders have the real privilege of interacting with the Job Seekers one-to-one. Everyone works together to make sure every Job Seeker feels welcome and comfortable. I love how we all work together to make it happen. We are the hands and feet and different parts but we all work together from our strengths to make it work.

My brother in Tennessee was talking to his Customer Service rep in Atlanta. He had worked with her for several years. As soon as she told him her department was being let go, he told her of RUMC Job Networking. Not too often do you get referrals out of state! She came and brought a co-worker and we became old friends instantly. She has come to visit our church and even came back after she got a job to see us one more time.

I really enjoy being a part of such a worthy ministry. I have a small part, but it is a necessary part that makes job networking run a little smoother. It is part of my "Martha" mentality to serve, fix, organize and mother. Helping with the dinner part of the Job Networking Ministry is a good fit for me. I have also enjoyed volunteering with my husband. Now when we talk about Job networking, it is a two way conversation and not him telling me how things went. It is a nice way to stay connected after the empty nest arrives.

Donna Litton:

I am a volunteer leader at RUMC Job Networking Ministry and have been a member since 1999. After college I began working as an accountant, then raised three children and later became the owner of the LittonGroup, LLC; which provides career management software and training for large organizations and individuals. My husband, Jay, and I have been married for 27 years. We have three children and one daughter-in-law.

I can be reached at donna@littongroup.com.

Neal's Story

I have been a member of Roswell United Methodist Church and the Bereans Sunday School class for 27 years. During the first 26 years I had never been asked to speak to our class. And when I think back about all the people in our Sunday school class, I think almost all of them had been asked to speak. I've also been involved with Job Networking for eight years, as a greeter and as a Table Host. And during this whole time I had never been asked to speak. I've known Rusty Gordon for 25 years and he speaks almost every other week. Never once has he asked me to speak.

But several months ago, a bank, in which I was a Director and had helped to start, entered bankruptcy, losing almost 400 million dollars. Within two weeks I received a phone call from the leaders of my Sunday school class and from Job Networking asking me to speak. I thought they wanted me to speak about Matthew, Mark, Luke or John. Or maybe even Romans. No, they wanted me to talk about the bank failing.

Now I don't know if these people who asked me to speak thought that anyone would learn anything from me, or they just knew everyone would feel better about their own situation!

A couple of years ago I went to a Prayer breakfast and heard Wayne Huizenga's son speak. Wayne started Waste Management, Block Buster Video and several other Fortune 500 companies. His son said the only reason he was asked to speak that day was because of his wealth, but he was glad he could use his wealth to share his faith. I guess you could say I'm glad I could use my failures to share my faith.

Before I began my speech at Job Networking I did a little research. I asked everyone there to pretend that it was Sunday morning and they were sitting in a beautiful church, the music had been wonderful, and they had just heard an inspiring message. I told them if they were Baptist they had just heard 13 verses of "Just as I Am." Then I asked everyone that claimed to have faith to raise their hands. Almost everyone did.

I then asked everyone to pretend they were at Job Networking, they were sitting in a room with several hundred unemployed people, and an old fat guy was up front trying to speak. But all they could think about was how they were going to pay their mortgage or rent, pay their car payment, pay their health insurance, pay their utility bills, or maybe pay tuition for a child in college. Or perhaps they were wondering if they were ever going to get a job interview.

It was my faith that got me through.

I then asked everyone to raise their hand if they had faith that they were going to get that great job they had always wanted. There were a lot fewer hands to go up.

What we found out with our research is that most of us have a lot of faith on Sundays, but it is Monday through Saturday where we need help.

Christianity is based on FAITH. That's it FAITH.

And how can we say we have faith on Sunday, believing in a God most of us have never seen when Monday through Saturday we don't even believe in the person we see in the mirror.

In Hebrews 11:1 it says, "What is Faith? It is the confident assurance that what we hope for is going to happen. It is the evidence of things we cannot yet see." When we think back at all the worries and stresses over the last several months, did we have faith? Did we have the "confident assurance that what we hoped for was going to happen?"

I remember Jack Nicklaus said one time that before he hits the ball he sees it going in the hole? Is that faith? Jack had the confident assurance that what he hoped for was going to happen. I would say that Jack had faith.

How many of us have that kind of faith?

This faith stuff is pretty neat. It's not just about getting to Heaven. It's about getting through today or getting through the week. Or getting that job we've always wanted. It's getting everything out of life that God intended.

Eight years ago I joined nine other local Christian businessmen to start a bank. It was going to be a faith based bank. We made the decision to pray before every meeting and to tithe our profits. We became one of the fastest growing banks in the country. We were making over a million dollars a month and we were giving 10% back to the community. We took the bank public a few years ago and the stock ran up almost 700 percent. And two years ago we received one of the best ratings you could get from the FDIC. God had really blessed us.

And then a year and a half ago, customers stopped making payments on their loans. Each month was worse then the last. We were loosing millions of dollars a month. It got so bad that seven of the ten directors resigned, with one having a heart attack.

Of the three of us that stayed, one had two strokes and the other spent several weeks in the hospital with stress related illnesses.

By default, I ended up with the task of dealing with the problems.

When we starting experiencing our problems I called the FDIC and told them I wanted to come down and tell them what we were doing to fix these problems. I was expecting to meet with one person. When I got there I noticed that a long list of people had signed in to meet with the same person. I thought I was going to have to wait a long time to meet with him. Little did I know that they were all there to meet with me.

We went into a big boardroom with one of those 50 foot tables. There were people from the FDIC and the State Banking authorities. They all looked at me and said, "Mr. Reynolds, did you have something to say." I knew then that things were going to be rough.

Everyday brought its own problems. We were written up in the Atlanta Business Chronicle, the Atlanta Journal and we were even featured on Good Morning America as a bank that was going to fail. That was not a good morning. I had to go to one of the bank branches to deal with the employees and the customers who were coming in to withdraw their money.

But the worst thing I had to deal with was the uninsured depositors. A couple of months before we were being taken over, I asked for a report on how many deposits were not insured by the FDIC. I found out we had $100 million in uninsured deposits. I got a list of all the depositors and went through every one of them. I was shocked when I found out many of these were friends, members of my church, and ministries that were part of my life. All I could think about was all these people loosing a hundred million dollars. Try sleeping after thinking about that!

Fortunately, at the end, my prayers were answered. A large regional bank agreed to buy all our uninsured deposits.

When I look back at all that happened this past year, it was my faith that got me through. It was my faith, my friends, my family, my small group, my Sunday School Class and my church.

I received sympathy cards from many of my friends. I told them the next time I loose $400 million I don't want a card; I want a casserole…a sweet potato casserole.

In James 1:3 it says, "For when your faith is tested, your endurance has a chance to grow. So let it grow, for when your endurance is fully developed, you will be strong in character and ready for anything."

Are you ready for anything? Are you ready for a bank to fail? Are you ready for your life savings to be wiped out? Are you ready to loose a job? Are you ready for a death in your family?

Neal Reynolds:

I am the husband of Jan and father of Matt and Lauren. In the last two years I lost a bank, my savings, my mother and my 101 year old grandmother. And my daughter got married. But God has blessed me more than I could have ever imagined. Job Networking has given me an opportunity to share my Faith and optimism for the future.

Pat's Story

In 2001, I started volunteering in the Job Seekers Ministry. Through all these years of involvement, I have been fortunate to be gainfully employed as an Employee Benefit Account Executive. What drove me to volunteer for this ministry?

After the birth of my daughter in 1987, I started attending RUMC with my son who was three years of age, old enough for Sunday school. Every Sunday I dropped him off at Sunday school while I attended worship in the sanctuary. Every Sunday in worship, I heard the words "Prayers, Presence, Gifts and Service." I was handling the Prayers, Presence and Gifts but felt my Service was lacking. So, I started teaching Sunday school to fill that void. Once my children grew to middle school age, I learned quickly that teaching Sunday School for middle schoolers was just not in me. The time had come for me to find another avenue of volunteer service.

Many come alone and are very lost not knowing what to expect.

Sitting in worship one Sunday morning, I noticed that this morning had been dubbed Volunteer Sunday. Jay Litton stood in front of the sanctuary and explained to us the Job Networking Ministry. He emphasized the need for volunteers for the Industry Guide Program. An Industry Guide didn't even have to attend meetings! As a mother of two active teens and holding a full time job, this program sounded like a no brainer to me: take one phone call from a Job Seeker once every two weeks. Sign me up!

A couple weeks later, I was invited to one of the Job Seekers meetings. I was encouraged to visit "just to see how the program works." Good idea! This way I would know what went on at these meetings. Hook, line and sinker, he got me. I attended the following meeting and have volunteered ever since.

Upon arriving at my first visit, I found John Harper greeting the Job Seekers. Inside the meeting room at a table two women (Debbie and Julie) signed in the Job Seekers, had them make name tags, and gave out information. The place was alive with energy. I saw Jay running around talking to everyone, just as he continues to do at all meetings now. Immediately I recognized that they could use some additional assistance.

Volunteering made me realize that although I was gainfully employed, one never knows when one could be in the same situation as Job Seekers. It is important to network, whether employed or not. Having networking skills may help me one day if I am in a job search. In the mean time, I am able to assist others by connecting people in need. I have even benefited by employing our Job Seekers at the company where I work.

Job Seekers appreciate our volunteers just being there for them. Many come alone and are very lost not knowing what to expect, where to go, or what to do. Having a smiling face to greet them helps them feel comfortable. We point the Job Seekers in the right direction and explain all that is available. This also eases their anxiety.

I started out being an Industry Guide, and still serve in that capacity. However, along the way, I added the responsibility of assisting with the set up before the meetings, greeting Job Seekers as they arrive, providing off site resume review, contact labels and communication, and coordinating the resume review line. The program started out with no money. The church did not budget any funds for this ministry. Somehow coffee and cookies appeared at each meeting. Signs were donated (most made by volunteers). Name tags for volunteers were donated and additional ones made as new volunteers came.

As the ministry grew, so did the recognition. We now have divided the responsibilities into categories to organize the flow better. Growing from 75 Job Seekers to 250 was a huge challenge, but we managed.

On a daily basis, I refer Job Seekers to this program by forwarding our meeting announcements, handing out and posting RUMC Job Networking business cards and just getting out the word that this ministry is there to help during their time of need. There are many older Job Seekers who have not experienced being out on the market for many years who need guidance. At the other end of the spectrum are those college graduates who are so tied into technology, they often do not have the skills or understandings that are a must in this market, such as the ability to network effectively.

One of the aspects of this ministry is pure "networking." Job Seekers who come to our meetings are almost forced to learn the skill of "networking." People outside of this ministry often ask me, "Does the ministry work in getting jobs for those seekers?" My response is that we are not there for the Job Seeker to become gainfully employed, which surprises them. We are there to provide support and tools for the Job Seeker in a Christian setting and to encourage them not to be alone during this time but to include God in their search.

Pat Holt:

I have attended/been a member of RUMC since 1987. My career has been focused in the field of Employee Benefits for the past 30 years. I currently volunteer my time for the RUMC Job Networking Ministry, involved in our neighborhood Home Owner Association, Class Manager for South Forsyth Jazzercise as well as participating in Jazzercise, and working on my CEBS certification. I have been married for 27 years and have two grown children.

Gary's Story

Industry Guide Program Leader

After graduating from Rutgers University in 1978 with a BS in Biology, I decided to pursue a military career and joined the Navy to fly airplanes. I was a Naval Officer and Navy Pilot for 17 years. When I left the Navy in 1995, I went through my first job and career transition. Before that, I had never had to look for a job.

When I began the transition from the active duty Navy world to the business world, I discovered it was a huge challenge. I had a lot to learn about career transition and job search.

Through my military network and friends I became aware of the West Point Society of Atlanta, an organization that helps former military officers make a successful transition to the business world. Through the West Point Society, I went through an in-depth career transition workshop and learned about the current techniques and skills for writing a resume, networking and interviewing. I also learned about and took part in several other free job search organizations at that time including "Seekers" and St. Jude's Church Job Transition workshops.

Through these organizations and their training I gained the knowledge to write an attention grabbing resume and learned how to interview successfully. As a result, I landed my first job in the business world as Director of Information Technology for a software company located in the Perimeter area of Atlanta. During my Navy career, I had learned about wide area networks and had managed a team of information technology professionals. I was able to leverage that experience to obtain this position.

In a little over a year, the Dot Com bust caused my company to go through a difficult financial period which resulted in a large layoff. My position was eliminated. Once again, I used the job transition skills I had learned to successfully network and land a position as Manager of Information Systems for National Linen Service. A couple of years later I decided that Information Technology was not the career path I wanted. I decided to make a change.

I discovered that it was the perfect place for me to share my skills and knowledge.

A good friend of mine offered me the opportunity to try Executive Recruiting with Andersen Consulting (now Accenture) and I really enjoyed it. I traveled to major cities across the U.S., sourcing and interviewing executive candidates in Finance and Accounting, Marketing, Public Relations, New Media and Professional Services. I went on from Andersen Consulting to hold Recruiting leadership roles with Global Crossing Telecommunications, AT&T and Comcast. In addition, I also had the opportunity to work for Spherion Corporation's Outplacement Division providing outplacement consulting services and teaching people displaced from down sized organizations how to find a new job. Then in 2003, I partnered with a friend of mine to build a recruiting consulting company called Talent Connections. Through these experiences, I mastered the skills of writing resumes, networking and interviewing from both the Job Seeker's and the employer's point of view.

In 2002 I became a member of Roswell United Methodist Church and within a year felt a tug on my heart to volunteer to use the skills and abilities I was blessed with to give back to others. I started by volunteering to teach 4th and 5th grade Sunday school.

This was an amazing experience and I think I got more out of it than the kids did! Then I heard about the RUMC Job Networking Ministry and attended a meeting to see what it was all about. I discovered that it was the perfect place for me to share my skills and knowledge of recruiting and job transition to help people in need. I attended meetings for about six months as a fill-in volunteer helping wherever needed. Over time I felt the desire to help out even more, so I jumped in and said, "I would really like to take on more responsibility here. How can I help?"

The answer was, "Well, why don't you take over the Industry Guide Program and work on improving it."

I did. Up to that point, we had 80-90 Industry Guide volunteers maintained in a spreadsheet in no particular order or organization. I realized there were several areas for improvement and began restructuring the Industry Guide Program. First, I rebuilt the Industry Guide database, reorganizing all the Industry Guide volunteers by industry. Then I created an Industry Sign and sign up sheet for each specific industry. This enabled Job Seekers to quickly find the industries they were interested in and sign up with Industry Guides in those industries. As a result, the Industry Guide process at the meetings was faster and more efficient. The positive response from the Job Seekers was tremendous. I continued to manage the Industry Guide program for three years and made additional improvements along the way.

Then, in 2008 as a result of the Recession, within one month the Job Networking meetings went from having around 100 Job Seekers to having 300+ Job Seekers at every meeting. We quickly realized that the current number of 80+ Industry Guide volunteers would not be enough to meet the increased number of Job Seekers we were receiving. To obtain some help with long-term planning and to increase the number of volunteers to meet the need, I formed an Industry Guide Leadership Committee which includes me and two other experienced Industry Guide volunteers. With the help of this committee, we restructured how the program was run. We increased the number of Industry Guide volunteers from 80 to

150 and created two new documents; (1) How to Start an Industry Guide Program and (2) A Guide for Industry Guides. These documents helped us to standardize some of our processes, created training for new Industry Guide volunteers and provided tools to help other churches or groups start an Industry Guide Program.

During the past couple of years we have received numerous accolades and praises from Job Seekers for the Industry Guide Program and how much it has helped them in their job search.

It has truly been a blessing and a wonderful journey to be a part of the RUMC Job Networking Ministry. To see this ministry grow and evolve to meet whatever the challenge or obstacle and observe firsthand the tremendous positive impact it has had on the success of numerous people in finding new jobs and careers is nothing short of God's miracle. I am honored and humbled to be a part of this life changing organization!

Gary Shaar:

I am a Volunteer Leader for the RUMC Job Networking Ministry and I lead our Industry Guide Program. I have over 12 years experience in contract recruiting and executive search and over 20 years in government and corporate leadership roles. I have also provided career transition and job search advice to individuals for six years. I currently own my own executive recruiting company (Gary Shaar & Associates, Inc.) and provide contract recruiting consulting services for client companies.

I can be reached at garyshaar@comcast.net.

Michael's Story

Why We Serve – A Story for Job Networking at RUMC

Let's start with an introduction. I have been a member at Roswell United Methodist Church for just over seven years. I came to RUMC on a profession of faith, more on that a little further down the page. I came to Georgia nine years ago for a job at Colonial Pipeline Company. Funny story about that….at my last job down in Miami, Florida I was Vice President of Technology for a small start-up firm. As it would happen I was in a board meeting one afternoon in July and we were reviewing the company finances and product strategies. We reported to the board that we would reach profitability, assuming we could obtain a 90% market penetration in the U.S. This news didn't seem to concern the other officers, and I being an IT guy and not an MBA, somehow did not believe that a little start-up in Miami could get 90% of any market to sign on the dotted line. Turns out I was correct. But I was blessed. After I returned to my office that same afternoon, I listened to a message on my voice mail from a recruiter looking for an IT leader to come to Atlanta.

The move to Roswell, Georgia followed. Eighteen months later I learned that I was going to be a father and the blessings continued. Our little family was in the midst of abundance. What was driving all this? One cool fall day I started to get the message. We were at a craft fair in old town Roswell ducking from tent to tent as cold rain fell. In one tent there was an artist who crafted metal sculptures from wrought iron scrap, and one of his pieces in particular caught the eye of my wife and me. It was a cross. The piece was about 40 inches high with a patina of orange rust and it was clear in a moment why we were brought to Roswell. We brought the cross into our home and invited Christ into our household.

We have been brought together at a special and trying time, to meet a tremendous need

Within a week we began the journey of finding the right church for raising our soon to be baby girl. As an IT guy, I listened to many online sermons from local churches and in September 2002, heard Mike Long preach concerning the anniversary of the 9/11 disaster. Over the internet his passion and empathy poured over Donna and me. The theme of this sermon was to fight evil with love. We had found our church home. Since that day this church has become part of my fabric and I hope that in some small part there is a thread of me amongst the white plaster.

When we joined RUMC the pastor asked us if we will support God's church at Roswell with our gifts, presence, prayers and service. The gifts part is easy enough, or at least it should be for those blessed to live in this community. Presence means coming to church every Sunday, even when it rains: check. Prayers…well that's new to a rookie, but I could work on it. Service… now what can I do in service for God's church and people? Luckily, the good people of RUMC made that pretty simple. Fairly quickly after joining the church in November of 2002, my wife and I received a service catalog, describing the ministries at RUMC. Job Networking seemed to be a good way to venture into this service responsibility. Within two days of filling out a service commitment card, Jay Litton called me, "Just stop by next Monday, and we'll show you the ropes."

Two things stuck with me from my first night of serving: The first was David's coaching on how to welcome folks in, "Smile, shake people's hands and introduce yourself. Make folks feel at home this is a tough time for people."

The second lesson came during the meeting. We had a small group that night around the holidays, maybe 20 people. So, we had an open discussion session. The conversation turned to finding good leads and getting past all the barriers between candidates and the interview. Well, I spoke right up. I've hired dozens of professionals. I know what this job seeking thing is all about. So, I offered about a half a dozen methods, feeling good all the while that I could provide the quality advice that would get people to the hiring manager. My pride swelled for all of 32 seconds, when one of the Job Seekers responded to my brilliance, "I've done all those things and more, but I'm 58 years old and haven't gotten an interview in a year. What else can I do?" This was a glimpse down the path of faith.

Reality is that any one of us can only do so much on our own. I quickly saw that I was not the one who could hire every person, make every contact and provide all those I met with comfort. But through faith and through the community of servants at Roswell we could be the conduit through whom God acts. He comforts. He Guides. He directs His outpouring of love and understanding. When I interact with Job Seekers at the meetings or as an Industry Guide I am reminded at once how little I can do, but how much God does through his people.

We offer so many services through this ministry. One of the greatest revelations I had four years ago came when a Job Seeker and I were talking about his search and the circumstances around the layoffs at his former employer. He spoke about the outplacement service with which he was working and stated that the counselor directed him to our program. What struck me then was the level of professionalism and talent we have been blessed with in this ministry. From the resume review, to the interview coaching; from the speakers to the greeters and from table leaders to the Industry Guides, there is an outpouring of talent brought together with a minimal budget; all working out of a passion for service. However, even with the high quality programs and products, I believe the greatest service we provide is a base level care for people in need. If Job Seekers ever doubt that they are loved, all they need to do is walk into this ministry.

One last word on why I serve. Who would not want to serve with a team of heroes like God has assembled at Roswell? The talents of the people that surround the program are truly awesome. Anyone who has ever had the privilege to be greeted by John Harper knows the love he pours out with every greeting and every prayer. Anyone who has shared stories with a true American hero, Richard (Dick) Fritz, gains an understanding of his sacrifice and caring for his fellow man and his church. Anyone who has seen Katherine Simons move mountains by her will and spirit is inspired to go and do. And anyone who has experienced the compassion and teaching of Jay Litton has been inspired to tell their own story that will WOW their audience. And there are so many more talents and people serving and inspiring not just on Monday nights, but continuously sparking hope and sharing love to the hurting. We have been brought together at a special and trying time, to meet a tremendous need in a little corner of a place called Roswell.

Why do I serve? How could I not?

Michael Dubois: Michael's bio information is incorporated into his story.

Melton's Story

A Real Industry Guide

I graduated from Georgia Tech with a degree in General Management in 1972 and followed that with a MBA in Marketing from Georgia State in 1980. In between Georgia Tech and Georgia State, I was in the Army.

I actually entered Georgia Tech in the fall of 1968 as an Industrial Engineering (IE) Major. After two short quarters of stumbling through freshman calculus, chemistry and graphics, I was on academic probation. Flunking out of college in the 1960's provided a unique opportunity offered by the federal government to go on an all expenses paid trip to Viet Nam. Unlike most of my counterparts, I was not against the war in Viet Nam. I just wanted to graduate from college first and go on active duty as an officer.

One of the best things that Georgia Tech prepared me for was how to handle adversity. I had to make an early career decision during my freshman year—flunk out of school and go to Viet Nam or change majors to Industrial Management (IM—now referred to as the *"M Train"* at Tech). It was actually an easy decision. However, it was tough to admit to myself that I couldn't graduate as an IE Major. I had graduated 7th out of my high school class of 210. This was not supposed to happen to me, but it did.

My father graduated from Georgia Tech with a Mechanical Engineering Degree in 1933. He knew what I was going through and supported my decision, which made it infinitely easier for me. This was one of my father's many gifts to me.

While at Tech, I was in Army ROTC, played on the Varsity Tennis Team and was an active member of my fraternity, Alpha Tau Omega. My interest in ROTC was not accidental.

My father was Robert Lee Hood, Jr. He was named for my grandfather, who was, ironically, named for Robert E. Lee. Robert Lee was a common name in the South in the 1880's after the War Between the States. So, my father also was named after Robert E. Lee.

As a retired Colonel, my father frequently took us to the Officers Club at Fort McClellan, Alabama, for dinner and bingo. Fort McClellan was only a few miles from where I grew up in Anniston, Alabama. The Viet Nam War was in high gear during the late 1960's, and you either went to college or went to Viet Nam after high school. So, I always thought that I would go into the Army after graduating from college.

Building your personal network is a lifelong endeavor.

When I say that I was in the Army, I was not just in the Army. While at Tech, I accepted a two-year Army scholarship starting with my junior year. Along with my ROTC scholarship, I was also able to choose the Corps of Engineers as my branch in the Army. I thought that this would provide me with some meaningful construction management experience. It just didn't work out that way.

The Corps of Engineers has two entirely different groups: one that is responsible for managing and maintaining all the rivers, streams, harbors and coast lines along with all public dams and levees and the Combat Engineers. I was a Combat Engineer Officer. The mission of the Combat Engineers is to support the combat units—the infantry and armor units.

My first and only assignment in the Army was with the 1st Cavalry Division located at Ft. Hood, Texas. Since I was fascinated with Civil War History, I researched the background for General John Bell Hood, for whom Ft. Hood was named. It turns out that General Hood was the Commanding General of the Confederate Army, who was responsible for defending Atlanta during the Civil War. As you all know, General Sherman defeated the Confederate Army that was defending Atlanta, which ultimately was the catalyst for ending the Civil War.

So, I was Lieutenant Hood at Ft. Hood, and my father was named for Robert E. Lee. It wasn't difficult for me to convince most of my contemporaries that I was "distantly" related to General John Bell Hood.

I arrived at Ft. Hood, Texas in February 1973 after completing the Engineer Officers Basic Course (EOBC) at Ft. Belvoir, which was located in Alexandria, Virginia and Jump School at Ft. Benning, Georgia. I also arrived at Ft. Hood within a few weeks of the 1st Cavalry Division's return from Viet Nam. I hadn't gone to Viet Nam, but almost everyone that I was working with in the 1st Cavalry Division had just been to Viet Nam.

When we were out in the field on training exercises, my platoon was "attached" to either an infantry or armor company. Most of the time, we were utilized as an additional infantry platoon. We rarely built anything except minefields and barbwire fences.

When I was not in the field with my platoon playing war games, I was playing tennis two to three hours a day, and I played in every Army Tennis Tournament along with almost every other tennis tournament in Central Texas from 1973–1976.

After deciding to leave the Army in 1976, I accepted a sales position with Amoco Chemical in Dallas, Texas. In 1978, I received a promotion, which included relocation to Atlanta, where I had always wanted to live. I eventually spent fifteen years working for Amoco in a variety of sales and marketing positions. I was happily married with two beautiful daughters.

However, successfully negotiating my way out of Georgia Tech, jumping out of perfectly good airplanes and playing competitive tennis did not prepare me for what happened next in my life. In January 1999, my boss, who had been both my mentor and tormentor, fired me after working for him for 15 years. His wife had taught our younger daughter, Julia, in pre-school. We had been friends. We had been out with them socially on a number of occasions. You can't imagine the shock and anger that I experienced. I did not sleep well for months thinking about all of this. I just could not believe that I had been fired. But I had and it happens to people every day.

I began the job hunting process. I was on a mission. I had faced adversity when I was a freshman at Georgia Tech. I had to admit defeat in tennis over the years and prepare for the next match. I felt like I could handle a new job search the same way.

In addition, I did have something else going for me. My kids were older, and I had my working, supportive wife, Lynn. We were going to be okay. The toughest part was telling all of my relatives, friends, customers and fellow Bereans Sunday School Classmates that I'd lost my job. The worst part about this was telling everyone that I had been fired, terminated, canned, etc....after 15 years. I had to park my ego at the door and admit another failure.

While painful, this is the number one thing that you have to do within the first two weeks of termination. Your family, friends and all of your business associates are your best allies. They can't help you if they don't know that you need help, and you need their help immediately after losing your job.

Despite all of my feelings of frustration and anger, I made myself join every networking group I could find as well as starting my own networking group. Showing up for these meetings was extremely difficult, but I did it.

At this time, RUMC had a small sales and marketing networking group that met every Monday morning at 9:00 a.m. in the parlor of the old church. There was also another Christian Networking Group called Job Seekers that met at the Houlihan's Restaurant at Perimeter every Thursday morning at 7:00 a.m. I forced myself to attend each of these meetings every week. After attending the meetings, I spent the rest of the day calling anyone that I could think of.

I used this opportunity to reconnect with friends from college—mostly fraternity brothers and good friends, who had successful careers or businesses. I also called all of my business friends, customers and suppliers—anybody whom I could think of at the time.

If you look at being unemployed as an opportunity to call guys you have not seen or talked with in 5-20 years, it is a neat experience. Most will be delighted to talk with you and give you 5-10 minutes of their time as well as a number of good contacts.

This process forces you to realize that you have to stay in touch with more people more often than you have ever done before. I routinely call five to six friends each week just to stay in touch. These could be guys that I worked with, hired or trained with. I also keep in touch with guys that I either grew up with or went to college with. Since this time, I've never stopped building my "Personal Network." Building your personal network is a lifelong endeavor. You may be doing it now. If you're not, now's a good time to start your "Personal Network."

In most cases, the guys that I called during my search would give me three to four contacts, which I would enter into my ACT Contact Manager for follow up. ACT was one of the first "Customer Relationship Management" (CRM) software tools, which was developed by Symantec. If you don't use some type of Contact Manager, consider using one now to track your phone calls and meetings. You have to be able to track and manage your contacts. If you have Microsoft Outlook, this is an excellent Contact Manager. At the time, I was using ACT and liked it better than Outlook. I spent the most time and the most attention with the contacts with the most promise. I did this routine for about five to six hours a day.

I discovered that I had to make this part of the job search a "Numbers Game." I had to make as many contacts as I could each day during my search, whether in person or over the phone. My daily goal was not to get a job, but to obtain three to four good contacts, with a secondary objective of obtaining a meeting or an interview.

On most days, I'd stop making calls around 4:00 p.m. and take a "Mental Health" break. If the weather were decent, I'd go out and hit tennis balls, golf balls or play nine holes. Regardless, I would do something fun which gave me a diversion from the job search grind.

At the end of three months, I had accumulated more than 300 new ACT contacts that I was following or categorizing for future follow up. I also had been on a number of interviews with a number of companies, including ones in both packaging and construction products businesses that I had the most interest. Two weeks later, (3 ½ months from termination), I had three job offers from these companies. I accepted one and restarted my sales and marketing career in April 1999.

At the conclusion of this process, I realized that I had received a great deal of help from both friends and other business associates, who I didn't know as well. In most cases, they took the time to try to help me. So, I made a promise to God and myself that I would always help anyone else who was ever looking for a job. Call it "Pay it Forward" or "My Deal with God."

I had taught Nursery School at RUMC—not well, but I would show up with my wife to tackle the three to six year olds that we inherited every week at RUMC. I tried teaching one of my older daughters' junior high Sunday School Classes—flunked out of that after the first class. Mission Trips to build anything never appealed to me. I hate anything more complicated than calling a plumber, carpenter or electrician to fix anything at our house. Teaching or going anywhere to help build anything wasn't one of my gifts.

Almost immediately after making "My Deal with God", Jay Litton appeared at our 11:00 AM service at RUMC and asked for "volunteers for Industry Guides", people interested in helping others find a job. I ran him down after the service to tell him that I wanted/had to be an "Industry Guide." While I wasn't good at other things, I'd become pretty good with conducting a job search.

At the time, we never talked about the rest of the story, but he signed me up anyway. After all, he needed volunteers. My sense was that Jay was looking for a "Few Good Men."

Since 1999, I have changed jobs several more times due to reorganization or termination, and I have used the same process that I have just outlined to gain other jobs and start over again.

It just took me a while to find my gift. I know what it is like to be fired, terminated, down sized, etc. Because of these experiences, I have committed my spare time to helping anyone, anytime with anything relating to a job search.

That's my story.

Melton Hood:

I am Melton Hood, and I've been a sales and marketing manager for over 30 years. My wife, Lynn, and I moved from Dallas, Texas to Marietta, Georgia in the fall of 1978. We have been members of Roswell United Methodist Church (RUMC) for over 30 years. We also were among the first couples to join the Bereans Sunday School Class. Most of our best friends are our class mates, whose children have grown up together as "Berean" Babies. I've been married for 34 years and have two adult daughters. I'm currently a National Sales Manager for Henkel Corporations' Consumer and Professional Adhesives Group. I can be reached any time at MWHood@bellsouth.net .

Barbara's Story

From Having a Life Touched, to Touching Lives

I have volunteered with RUMC Job Networking for almost three years, providing Resume Review. People ask why I've stayed with it so long. I tell them the truth. Providing such a valuable, tangible service to people truly in need is extremely rewarding. Resume review is powerful for the Job Seeker and the volunteer resume reviewer. Job Seekers are so appreciative of the service and the fact that someone cares about helping them with their job search – they keep telling us how helpful it is to them to have a well-written resume! The volunteers appreciate the difference can make in another person's life in such a short time.

I started volunteering for this program because I benefited from another RUMC group: the Bereavement Support Group. I attended Bereavement Support Group meetings for several months after my father died. I wanted to thank RUMC for providing this group but didn't want to just write a donation check. I saw the Job Networking signs (the meetings happened to be on the same day of the week as the Bereavement meetings) and walked in one night and asked if I, as a corporate recruiter, could help in any way. I was pointed towards Resume Review and that's where I've been ever since. I now coordinate the Resume Reviewers as well as review resumes myself.

Reviewing resumes has been of even more importance to me, while I was unemployed the past several months. Many of our Job Seekers tell us that not being productive, not having something useful to do is one of the hardest things about being unemployed (aside from the financial aspects) – and it was the same for me. Being able to help others and be productive was so beneficial to me. This was just another example of volunteering being more helpful to the volunteer than the cause.

The volunteers know they're providing a valuable service and appreciate the difference they can make.

I think one of the most powerful aspects of Resume Review is that we review Job Seekers' resumes individually. Our resume reviewers are recruiters, HR professionals, resume writers – they know what hiring managers look for, what works on Internet job boards, common resume mistakes, etc. They are professionals. The Reviewer looks at the actual resume, writes comments, makes concrete suggestions, re-writes phrases, discusses format (font, margins, etc.) and style (no functional resumes, only chronological), etc. Job Seekers leave with a template of how to improve their resumes, not just some vague ideas.

I have seen many poorly written and badly formatted resumes as a corporate recruiter. I can look past that and see the candidate's skill set, but I know from experience that a lot of hiring managers cannot. We're truly helping Job Seekers because we assist them in showcasing their achievements in a polished and professional manner. Many people bring resumes that well-meaning friends have written for them or are using outdated formats. I am certain their resumes are not getting the attention of recruiters, HR, and hiring managers. With our assistance, we can increase the odds that the Job Seeker's resume will get forwarded to the person who can make the job offer.

Would You Like to Have Your Resume Reviewed?

Barbara Marks:

I coordinate the Resume Reviewers and the "Ask an Expert" Roundtable Speakers program for RUMC Job Networking. I have worked as a recruiter in the Atlanta area for the past 10 years. I have spent the majority of my career as a contract corporate recruiter, both on-site and virtual assignments. I do not attend RUMC (I'm Jewish) but assisting Job Seekers is very important to me. RUMC makes it possible for me to volunteer doing something I love (assisting Job Seekers) yet makes no religious demands of me and I really appreciate that.

Craig's Story

Growing through Service

I was born an overachiever; driven by nature and am a bit of a perfectionist. I began working at a trade at age 16 and by age 24 had obtained an advanced engineering education, worked full time in my profession and had been married for four years. Now at 62, I have actually experienced four very distinctly diverse careers, covering a wide range of experiences from staff engineering to the entrepreneurial world. For me, life in the workplace has been like running a race in a labyrinth. Trying to be the best employee, producer, leader, father, husband, and son while trying to figure out how to navigate the roadblocks every time I hit another dead end has made life interesting, challenging, frustrating and filled with learning experiences. I have known great successes and great failures in the marketplace and have often been challenged beyond anything I was able to handle. Yet, I find myself today having not only survived the workplace jungle, but richly blessed by the experiences and the challenges.

Being married 42 years to a pragmatic, energetic, enterprising and exciting lady (who has always had a much clearer picture of life's purpose and God's plans for living) has tempered and educated me as I hit each of life's challenging phases. Most importantly, she has always somehow managed to make sure that in whatever circumstance I found myself, I didn't forget that humility and faith would be the source of my solutions.

You've met the lady of my life, since she's the author of this book. So you will understand that when her passions get going, she has an amazing ability to draw people and resources to her cause. She also has an innate ability to see clearly the gifts that others possess (that often they themselves do not see) and to be able to encourage them to put these gifts to work. I have always been one of those first people she called when the challenge arose. She also has always been able to see much more practically than I, how my gifts can be best applied. So, it can be no surprise that as she began to see the awesome power of people coming together to serve Job Seekers, that she drew me into the call.

It turns out that the last of my career experiences was to partner with my wife in a growing healthcare staffing company, which she had started as a small business nearly 20 years earlier. With upwards of 40 internal employees and nearly 1,000 temporary staff, this experience gave me some rather extensive and practical knowledge of many HR functions. When Katherine recognized the need to grow the Resume Review area, I was one of the first to be called to serve.

At first in resume review we had little direction on what to do. It was obvious that Job Seekers really desired to receive critical input on their resumes. Those of us who volunteered to review resumes simply met one-to-one with Job Seekers and give them our thoughts. Our team of volunteers has always been diverse; however, each possesses extensive experience in the hiring process, generally in HR or recruiting. But, each of us approaches the review quite differently, reflecting our gifts and our experiences.

When I first started, I was not sure how I could best help. I am not a trainer, counselor, HR expert, or educated in any of these areas. I simply have spent nearly 40 years as a hiring manager and have reviewed more resumes then most people have seen in a lifetime. And I was always in a position in which I was held accountable for the success of my hire. So, I started by doing a lot of listening and questioning, rather then giving a lot of instructions, re-write and/or samples.

I discovered fairly quickly that most Job Seekers came in with very ineffective resumes and a grateful desire for the opportunity to have someone give them honest feedback. I explained to them how I would react as a hiring manager if I received their resume. Often, this would lead very quickly to career discussions and the personal issues people were dealing with in their search.

Sometimes it just requires getting them to see it. When that happens, the road to success is started.

I further discovered that most Job Seekers didn't really understand how their resumes would be used (or viewed). More importantly, they simply did not understand their own goals, gifts, successes, or how to present themselves with value. Most had not thought through how they needed to approach the job search process systematically. The result was that they were confused, frustrated and directionless and their resumes reflected that.

I chose simply to provide honest feedback while encouraging the Job Seekers to identify their skills and their accomplishments from their work years. I helped them see their value in the workplace and guided them in how to present that value in their resumes. I felt that I was doing little, yet almost without exception, those with whom I spoke left with such a sense of peace and gratitude that I would depart after my hour of service, knowing that I had helped someone.

How often do you spend one hour doing what comes naturally and walk away repeatedly with grateful and positive feedback from those you work with? From day one, even with my fears and my inadequacy, I would leave this resume review time refreshed and personally satisfied that the best of me had been used, someone had been helped and I had received a grateful, "thanks."

In the years since that first "fearful" night for me, I have refined my process and improved my style. But, for me this continues to be a time to allow the Job Seeker to expose their struggles and then to refocus their thinking about themselves in a way that makes them proud of who they are and what they have done. We also work hard at getting the individual to identify clearly how their unique gifts, work experiences and practical accomplishments make them valuable to the marketplace. We then spend time on ways to present these "discoveries" in the resume and showing how they can make potential employers see the value that they bring.

In this process, truthfulness is absolutely essential, even when it hurts. Sometimes we need to be blunt, because people have a tendency not to see themselves clearly. I have had to tell people that they need to give up on the direction they are presenting in their resume and "repackage" themselves for a new future. But, almost without fail, what I see in the Job Seekers are individuals with skills and talents that can be used effectively in the marketplace. Sometimes it just requires getting them to see it. When that happens, the road to success is started and each of us is blessed by the experience.

I wish every interview was a total success. Unfortunately there are those times when people come in with the wrong motives or expectations. In these times, the best I can do is to acknowledge my limitations, encourage them in who they are, and express our united desire to help them in this process. Fortunately, these situations are rare and they are overshadowed by the positive experiences I have discussed already.

Let me also comment on those experiences where people come in with great resumes. This is actually a fun time, because most of our time is spent in encouragement. Those sessions have both of us excited about what is ahead.

Another area of personal satisfaction that has come from this experience is my personal knowledge and growth. Why is it a surprise, that when we give unconditionally, we end up getting more in return? Through this experience (which started without my having any identifiable skills for the review) I have grown in my knowledge and in my understanding of my own personal skills. I actually have been motivated to grow in knowledge and experience of resume writing, counseling, presentation, etc. I have further developed an interest in the job networking process and have found myself as a conduit to help others know of the resources available, even down to helping initiate a new Job Networking Ministry in Europe. Participating in this program at RUMC has connected me with an amazing group of quality volunteers, who teach me regularly about all areas of life, from which I can grow. It is amazing what happens when you surround yourself with quality people who give of themselves for the benefit of others.

We all come out as winners.

Craig Simons:

I have been a member of Roswell United Methodist Church since 1982 and have been active in all areas of its leadership and ministries. I have spent over 40 years in the marketplace, most in leadership roles in large corporations, with the last years supporting my wife in her entrepreneurial venture that we eventually sold. Today, I balance most of my time between serving in my family, community and church organizations. I am still consulting to and involved with several companies. I listen and learn. I currently work with Crown Financial Ministries, by reaching out to other people and nations in need. I can be reached at craigsimons@ddsstaffing.com.

Nancy's Story

Reflections from a Resume Reviewer

After relocating to Atlanta from Minneapolis for a promotion with a company, I found I was laid off. Having only been in Atlanta for two and one-half years, I really didn't have the networks or contacts I had made in Minneapolis. After spending some time trying to figure out where to go and what to do, I decided to stay in Atlanta.

Being single, I knew I had to make contacts and find a job quickly. Earlier in my career, I had been employed as a Career Consultant, so I knew the importance of building a network. I put my resume together, searched online and started networking with the people I knew.

Through my network, I learned of a church called RUMC that provided job seeking assistance. I attended the program, I felt at home with the approach and I found the job seeking information extremely useful. The volunteers were sincere. I felt welcomed.

Over the months, I continued to participate in this program. My network grew tremendously and I found contract work as a Career Consultant at a few universities and government agencies. Eventually I landed a job as a Senior Staffing Manager in a multinational software and computer consulting company. I consider this to be a direct result of all the contacts and support I received from RUMC.

Once employed, I was asked to volunteer on the Resume Review Team and I have been volunteering over 5 years now, currently as Resume Reviewer and Roundtable Discussion Leader. During this time, I helped to coordinate some social activities for the volunteers. Being a volunteer, I recognized how important it is for a ministry to make sure volunteers are taking time to get to know each other. We depend on each other to provide the best service to the Job Seekers. These Job Seekers struggle emotionally and physically. They work many hours and often do not see the fruits of their labor. We need to be there for them. But at times, our energy as volunteers can be low and in order to be available to the Job Seekers, the volunteers need to be there for each other for guidance, fun and support.

I recognized how important it is for a ministry to make sure volunteers are taking time to get to know each other.

One thing I learned as a volunteer in this program is how critical it is to make sure the volunteers have an opportunity to get to know each other. We needed to plan some social activities just for the volunteers. They are our greatest asset and need to stay motivated. As a volunteer myself, I knew it was easy to show up and share my knowledge and expertise. But even volunteers, over time, can burn out. Usually, it is because there are not enough opportunities to socialize and interact. As a volunteer, you don't want to feel like you are going from one job to another. As a volunteer in the program, it is important for us to know each other and seek out each other's expertise.

In summary, there are many reasons I continue to participate as a volunteer. I really believe that this ministry provides an invaluable service to me, when I was in job transition and I wanted to "Pay it forward." Through my own experience as a Career Consultant, I witnessed the need to mentor and be mentored. I am very motivated to assist others in their job search and feel I can make a difference. Each Job Seeker is so appreciative. It makes volunteering a natural high. I really enjoy people and making a difference in their lives. In addition, being around other volunteers, who share the same values and participate in life fully, is very energizing and uplifting.

It seems to me that I have come full circle. A laid-off employee, relocating from Minneapolis, attends a job networking meeting, finds career coaching contract work, continues to volunteer and participate after landing full-time employment. Now, 5 years later I thoroughly enjoy being in service and regularly encourage others in similar life situations to join in the joy.

Nancy Schrempp:

I am a Volunteer at the RUMC Job Networking Ministry and a member of RUMC since 2005. I am currently employed as a Senior Resource Analyst (Staffing Manager) for a Global Software and Consulting Company. Prior professional experience includes work as a Career Consultant/Trainer, Continuing Education Director and Student Activities Coordinator at colleges and universities. I hold a MA in Adult Education. I managed two lay offs and one career transition throughout my work history. I consider myself a life long learner and truly value all the people and experiences I have encountered throughout my career.

Eric's Story

FAQ's while People Await a Resume Review

The company I was working for had just sold itself to a larger company. My wife was worried about the impact on us and suggested that the church had a program for Job Networking. I mentioned that a friend had a really good and smart process he was using. My wife asked, "If his process is so good why aren't you using it?" I went to the Job Networking meeting the next night.

I showed up 30 minutes early for the second meeting and volunteered to help. They had enough people greeting at the door and sent me down to the resume review line to help assist Job Seekers getting to the next available Resume Reviewer. I have been volunteering for over two years now.

Resume review ranges from 8-30 volunteers who in most cases look at 100's of resumes during their regular workday, then come to the our program and review some more. A line of people wait patiently to have their resume reviewed. I help control the line and the flow of people getting their review.

One of the standard questions I was getting asked every time was "Who are these people?" I eventually worked up a routine of the most frequently asked questions and tips. While the people await their turn, I just start a running commentary of all the information I have gathered during my last two years. I typically start with who the reviewers are and go from there. I include the problem of getting a review, where one person suggests making the font smaller and the next person that reviews your resume may suggest making the font larger. Resume preparation is not an exact science and there are many different schools of thought. So, I encourage Job Seekers to build their own Best Practices by asking "why?" for every suggestion. This will allow each individual to control all of the suggestions and use what is best in their circumstance. For example, if the reason for making the font larger is better than the reason for make it smaller, the Job Seeker will have a new Best Practice and make the change.

If his process is so good why aren't you using it?

Personally, I have been through three job transitions in the last three years. That is challenging but to have an outlet in which I can assist others in getting help and therefore feel useful provides my reward for the small time and effort required. The fact that I get an early shot at the home-made chocolate chip cookies is just a special bonus.

Eric West:

I am a Volunteer Leader at the RUMC Job Ministry and a member of RUMC. I have been married for 22 years. I also volunteer as leader of an IT Advisory Group that meets weekly. We have helped over 450 people with their job transition. I have 20+ years of technology experience, including geophysical, information technology, intellectual property, and telephony.

Darren's Story

God is an active God

I have learned that the only limitation to God's involvement in my life is my allowance. If I ask God to be involved, He will be.

It has also been my experience that once I ask Him, He effects immediate action. Normally this is through a whisper of guidance. But if I don't listen, He will give me a push.

Two years ago I was with a company in Orlando and through an acquisition I was given a promotion opportunity. To accept this promotion, I had to move to Atlanta. My new wife and I left behind our families and friends and made the move. A year later, I learned of another acquisition. My position was eliminated as a result. I was given the news of my pending dismissal eight days before Christmas. Two weeks before my last day, I learned my wife was pregnant.

It was a great way to get connected into the church and meet other members.

I dealt with many negative emotions after losing my job. How would I be able to support my new wife and my new family? What will the rest of my family think of me making this relocation just to be let go? How competitive was I in a new market? How will this change my life?

How will this change my life? The most difficult of the questions, but the most appropriate to be asked. I would learn later, that was the whole point…to change my life.

After the relocation, my wife and I discussed locating a church. I had grown up in the church and had always been a part of one, but had not been the active participant that God desired for many years. I was there in spirit, but not in body. God needed my body. He had a bigger role for me to play.

As I was beginning my job search we visited RUMC and met with a Pastor who directed me to the Job Networking leadership and the ministry. She offered that it was a great way to get connected into the church and meet other members, as well as helping me in my search. I tentatively made a trip one night and found myself warmly welcomed, while in the company of strangers facing similar situations. I left with gained knowledge. I was so pleased with how that church represented itself through the ministry that it led us to become members of that church. I took an immediate interest in the Job Networking Ministry and quickly became an active volunteer. I was asked to participate in a discussion on adding a dinner to Job Networking. I was moved that these people, to whom I was a stranger, would involve me in such a discussion.

God went to work in my life. I became a resume reviewer, then a Table Host at the Job Networking Ministry. My involvement led to an active role in the church. We've joined a Sunday School Class and I became the Programs coordinator for the class. My wife and I have participated with local ministries and Vacation Bible School. We are creating relationships and are looking forward to raising our family in the new church home.

I was out of work six months. I am now in a position that has re-energized my passion for my work, and though it was trying and frustrating, the experience of being out of work led me down a path I would never have ventured otherwise.

I am so amazed by God's purpose and all those things He does to drive His mission. I have learned three lessons from this experience.

- Sometimes God wants me somewhere else;

- If I'm not where He wants me to be, He will move me, whether by whisper or push;
- It is not about me.

God wanted me out of Orlando. He wanted me in Atlanta. He wanted me to be *right here, right now.* He is utilizing me as part of His grand mission. For what more could I possibly ask?

After being involved for several months, I created an email and sent to the members of the Job Networking Team sharing my story and letting them know how much it has meant to me. In that email, I included a few of the lyrics from a song by the Contemporary Christian band, Mercy Me. This song became so important to me during that transition time of my life. God gave me this song during that time and I wanted to share it with others.

Because I know God is an active God. And because I trust His purpose for my life, I pray the chorus of that song…

Give me joy, give me peace
Give me the chance to be free
Give me anything that brings you glory.
And I know they'll be days
When this life brings me pain
But if that's what it takes to praise you,
Jesus brings the rain.

Darren Shipp:

I am a technology executive that specializes in process engineering organizations for reduced expenditures, increased performance and streamlined operations. I am the author of the Integrated Requirements Development (IRD) and Requirements driven Agile Development (RdAD) methodologies for managing software development activities in organizations and industry recognized and published in the areas of requirements management and innovative people management. I currently hold the position of Vice President, Software Development at AutoVIN. My wife Kristina, son Dillon and dogs Maggie and Mandy live in John's Creek, Georgia.

Kay's Story

My Journey in Job Networking

I began working at RUMC over six and a half years ago and from the very beginning I have been working with Job Networking, in one capacity or another. For many years I merely handled the secretarial aspects of the job. I kept the database, prepared the attendance sheets for the meetings, sent out the agendas to those listed and made copies of data to be distributed at the meeting.

All that changed in August of 2009, when I was given the honor of becoming the staff person in charge of Job Networking. With this new position my responsibilities increased and I became much more involved with the whole process from beginning to end. Since this was one of the ministries within my responsibilities, I wanted to know as much as I could, so that I could do my best. I decided that I would attend one of the dinners, which are held prior to the meeting itself, and then attend the technical sessions. I felt sure by attending one dinner program and then the meeting that followed I would have a greater appreciation for all that was involved and be able to use that information to support this ministry.

Well, that was many months ago and that one experience has now grown into my participating as a Table Host every time a meeting is held. I thought I was very knowledgeable about what Job Networking was all about, but after attending that one meeting I was so in awe of what transpired that I found myself wanting to be a part of it. When I witnessed what happens between 3:00 p.m. and 9:00 p.m., it was just beyond one's imagination.

There are many different teams of volunteers who donate their time twice a month to this ministry. Just like it takes "A Village to Raise a Child" it takes many teams to run these two ministries. I say two, because prior to the meeting there are workshops taking place from 1:30 p.m. to 5:00 p.m. where special skill sets are offered to those people who are and have been without a job for days, weeks and months or longer. At 5:45 pm the Fellowship Hall becomes a safe haven for the 275 to 340 people who come to eat dinner and be spiritually fed by a guest speaker who brings Jesus into their lives for that short 45 minute period. The Table Hosts are there to lead discussions following the guest speaker presentation and to make sure that all those at that table feel welcome and encouraged in their time of need.

I found myself wanting to be a part of it.

The first night I led a table I was overwhelmed with the stories. I saw and heard the faith and hope in Job Seeker's faces and in their words. They expressed an overwhelming sense of gratitude for the people who welcomed them as they walked in, for the people who prepared the meals and those who filled their plates with food. They talked of how they felt hope after the minister said a prayer before the meal and then how they were touched by the words of the presenter. They were impressed by all the different classes and offerings available between the dinner and the meeting.

After hosting a table, I make sure to follow-up by sending an email or a phone call to all who were at my table. Some of the responses, that I get back, touch my heart in ways that mere words cannot express.

I am blessed to have a job in these tough times, but more than that I am blessed to have a job that I love to come to each day. I take my job very seriously and feel that each aspect of it is a special ministry that I have been called to do. On the second and fourth Monday of each month, after my day of work at the church, I am then anxious to volunteer as a Table Host. I guess for me, the big difference is that in the time that I serve I give of my heart to a very worthy cause.

When you attend one of these meetings and you look in the eyes of all the volunteers you get a glimpse of what grace is all about. Each and every one of us gets so much more than we give when we volunteer our time. My faith and trust in the Lord has been greatly influenced by all those that I come in contact with. I wish everyone could attend just one meeting and see the light of Christ that shines from all who minister to these Job Seekers. I am truly blessed and proud to be a part of this wonderful ministry.

Kay Elizabeth Holmquist:

I am the Facilities Administrator; Dave Ramsey Financial Peace Coordinator and Staff Contact for Job Networking at Roswell United Methodist Church. I have been blessed to be a part of the RUMC staff for over six years now. I have been a legal secretary for 10 years and a staffing coordinator for a major department store for three years. I am a member of St. Peter and St. Paul's Episcopal Church, where I serve as a Stephen's Minister, and a Lay Eucharistic Minister. I have served on the Secretariat of the Cursillo movement in the Atlanta area for five years. The true joy of my life is being married to my husband Ernie and being Mom to Tara, Timothy & Robby and "Grammie" to Taylor, Sysney & Tommy.

Mary's Story

Nudged in the Right Direction

A friend once told me that "sometimes God presents an opportunity to nudge you in a direction." That was certainly the case with me and Job Networking. I had never considered volunteering in this ministry area. I wasn't an HR Professional or a Recruiter so I really didn't think my spiritual gifts or background would be a good fit for this ministry. In June, 2008, all of that changed. A dinner was added to our Job Networking Ministry. This was to be a dinner, speaker and small group focused on helping Job Seekers develop their "spiritual resume." I was asked to help in the planning and coordinating of these dinners. I had been on staff at RUMC and we had planned, organized, and recruited volunteers for many programs and events during that time. I agreed to help organize the dinners but only for a few months and 18 months later I am still involved!

The response to the dinners has been amazing. Approximately 80 people attended our first dinner and we now average 300. We have never taken reservations for the dinner, and we always seem to have enough food and enough volunteers! I was invited to be part of this ministry and I then invited others, including my husband, Scott, and they in turn have invited others and now we have people calling to say "what can I do to help?" The Job Seekers even volunteer to help with the dinners and they continue to help even after they have found jobs. What a difference we can make when we reach out to each other!

In addition to coordinating the Table Host Team, I have had the privilege of being a Table Host and getting to know the Job Seekers, hearing their stories, praying with them and following up with them. My training as a Stephen Minister serves as a reminder to me that "God is the Cure-giver and we are the Caregivers." While I can't find jobs for these Job Seekers, I can be a Christian friend, a good listener and to serve as a reminder to them that there is a God who loves them and is walking beside them during this difficult time.

I realize that by saying "yes" to an invitation, I allowed God to use me.

I leave each Job Networking meeting touched by the Job Seekers whom I have met. I know that God has blessed me by giving me the opportunity to serve him in this ministry. I realize that by saying "yes" to an invitation, I allowed God to use me and equip me with what I needed to make just a small difference in someone's life and they in turn have made a difference in mine!

Mary & Scott Schaefer:

I, Mary, am a Volunteer Coordinator at the RUMC Job Networking Ministry and a member of RUMC since 2002. I have prior work experience at several United Methodist Churches including RUMC where I served as Director of New Members until May, 2007. My husband, Scott, is also a Job Networking Volunteer and together we offer Saturday morning devotionals at two Assisted Living Facilities. We have been married for 39 years. We have two married sons and on January 11th we were blessed by the arrival of a beautiful grandson.

Bob's Story

During worship, on the Sunday before Thanksgiving, 2001, our minister asked for volunteers to stand up and share briefly what they were thankful for. The year had been particularly horrible for me. I had changed jobs at the end of 1999. Shortly after beginning my new job, the company downsized. I was part of the downsizing. Fortunately, I found another job fairly quickly. Then much to my dismay another situation arose that found me without a job again!

I listened to a few share their moments of gratitude. Then I stood to share. I introduced myself and said, "I am thankful that God has given me so many opportunities to practice and hone my job interviewing skills this year." I felt that I had given a very positive spin to a very negative situation. Scattered chuckles rippled through the congregation as I took my seat.

Through all of that, I learned how difficult it was to re-invent myself, especially at that point in my life. Writing my resume, and then re-writing my resume, networking with family, friends, colleagues and peers, and honing my interviewing skills generated a lot of stress, not only for me but also for my family. Without a job, I felt as if I failed them. That added pressure to my search. I like to think that God knew that I would eventually use some of the skills that I learned along with gaining understanding of the angst that Job Seekers experience.

Shortly after my period of unemployment, Jan and I decided to become a team of real estate agents in the residential arena. We took the necessary courses and obtained our real estate licenses. During that process we also did our homework on where we wanted to concentrate our work. We learned how difficult it is to strike out on your own. We quickly identified the adjustments we had to make when we went to no income. I discovered that it takes a certain type of mindset to be able to be self-employed and to remain focused on work. In retrospect, I recognize this awareness also helps me in what I do in my role with Job networking.

Unemployment is an equal opportunity un-employer.

I was asked to join the RUMC Job Networking Ministry some 18 months ago. I really had to consider how I was going to fit another activity into my life. But it became clear to me that I had a lot of experience to offer the Job Seekers, those inside the corporate world as well as those who were self-employed. I remembered how difficult it was for me when I was unemployed. If I could be a servant to those in need, then that would be what I would do. I have never regretted a single moment as a volunteer and have expanded my role to include part time speaking. I come to each meeting to share and encourage. I leave having been encouraged as well.

Unemployment is an equal opportunity un-employer. It knows no boundaries, no age limitations or race. There are no color barriers. It strikes the poor and the rich alike. Men and women, white, Asian or black. When we gather together on Mondays, we have a mixture of all people, joined together by a loss. It is part of our role as Table Hosts to make sure that our guests know that they are not alone. There are a total of ten people at the table with whom they can relate. My responsibility is to facilitate the discussion at the table while helping everyone feel more comfortable.

While we eat, we introduce ourselves to one another. The Job Seekers tell what they have done in their careers and what they are looking for. The dinner speaker takes about fifteen minutes to bring his/her message to everyone. The speaker provides probing questions that we discuss at our individual tables.

I believe that this discussion segment is the most critical and insightful portion of the dinner program. Table Hosts are there to encourage meaningful discussion from all participants at the table. We gently guide the conversation so that it stays on point. If a lull occurs, we ask an individual, who might not have contributed, to give us his/her thoughts on the question. We have about fifteen minutes to discuss the message and questions. We rarely finish before the time ends.

The Job Seekers inspire me and encourage me as they open up and share meaningful, perhaps even personal feedback on the message of the night. I realize that most of them also have been encouraged by of our time together. That is so satisfying to me. Following the meeting, I send an email to each person at my table. I want them to know that I am thinking about them and that I am available for them. Most Job Seekers are amazed that a Table Host would take time to drop them a message, to check up on them. Some even respond and give us feedback on how they perceived the evening. I leave Job Networking at the end of the evening with a spiritual high, knowing that I saw a glimmer of hope in someone's eye, a nod of affirmation and perhaps a smile.

Bob & Jan Kashey:

My name is Bob Kashey and I am a volunteer Table Host and speaker for the Job Networking Ministry at Roswell United Methodist Church. My wife, Jan, also volunteers in this ministry. Together we are residential real estate agents.

Gale & Roger's Story

Dual Duty – Delighting in Both

The Greeter/Server Team is another element of Job Networking that evolved as the ministry grew and transitioned to better serve the growing number of participants. Because of the significant growth in the number of Job Seekers in early 2009, the ministry had to be relocated from the Dod (our youth facility) where it had been meeting for a number of years, to the church fellowship hall and nearby classrooms. In conjunction with this relocation, the decision was made to serve dinner as a part of the ministry.

Our initial responsibility with the ministry was that of "servers" for the dinner. There were six volunteers to help serve the meal. The first night approximately 80 joined us for dinner. There was an excitement about the crowd and some anxiety within our new volunteer group. But, all went like clockwork and we had plenty of food.

We want to continue the feeling of "special guests" for the participants.

At each subsequent meeting the number of participants grew and making the evening a special event for the job Seekers became more difficult. As the Greeter/Server Team discussed the challenges, we purposed to provide a very warm, personal and welcoming atmosphere to assure that each person would feel that they were special "guests" and not just one in the crowd.

Some of the changes made to enhance our ability to achieve our hospitality purposes were:

- Create a separate group of volunteers to focus on setting the tables, getting the room ready, greeting, seating, and serving the Job Seekers. We currently have 12-14 volunteers who serve at each Job Networking session.
- Assure that each Job Seeker is greeted and escorted to a table for seating. We want to fill the room starting with tables at the front. We position the volunteers in such a way that the guests are greeted, directed and finally seated at a table with a Table Host. We want to assure that they never feel alone as they find a table.
- Name tags are placed on each table and participants are encouraged to put them on prior to going for their meal. Volunteers are encouraged to call people by their names during the course of the evening.
- To avoid long lines and give more personal service we set up two food serving lines, as well as a beverage station and a desert station. We attempt to minimize the number of decisions the Job Seekers have to make by anticipating their needs and making it easy for them.
- After the meal is finished, the tables are cleared by Table Hosts and the volunteer greeters/servers. We want to continue the feeling of "special guests" for the participants.

Our goal for the Job Seekers is for them to feel they have been warmly welcomed, properly seated, joyfully served, called by name, and in all ways treated as a guest. When this happens it sets the stage for them to enjoy the rest of the program and anticipate good things happening during the remainder of the evening. Additionally they will know that we care and we care because God cares. We want to be conduits of God's love to each person who comes.

We have been especially blessed by being a part of the Greeter/Server Team. The team is made up of folks who have a passion for the Job Networking Ministry. A number started with the thought of just seeing what volunteering in this area was all about. They quickly found their niche in the program and realized the impact they can have by serving. We appreciate the flexibility of each volunteer to move into whatever needs to be done and see that it is done well. We have all been abundantly rewarded by the comments from the Job Seekers affirming that they truly felt welcome and were treated as special guests.

Gale & Roger Davis:

We are volunteer leaders of the Greeter/Server Team of the RUMC Job Networking Ministry. We have been members of RUMC since 1982 and have served in a number of capacities as volunteers and volunteer leaders. In addition, we both served on the staff of RUMC for approximately ten years where we were responsible for the area of Evangelism and New Members. We are very active in a large Sunday School Class and have been on numerous mission trips to Mexico, Peru, and to Katrina rebuilds in Mississippi. We were married in 1961, have three children and seven grandchildren. We can yell "Go Gators" and "War Eagle" with equal enthusiasm.

We can be reached at Rogale1@bellsouth.net.

Kathy & John's Story

We are Kathy and John Glankler. Since our marriage in 1981, we have lived in seven states and have been members of seven different United Methodist congregations. After returning to the great state of Georgia in 2004, we searched for a ministry opportunity in a church that needed our help. We also wanted to find a church where we enjoyed being part of the ministry.

Our active involvement in RUMC came about because of the friendship we made with Mary and Scott Schaefer. They were a huge part of our decision to join RUMC. In our new member class, Mary and Scott did a great job leading us. They also became good friends. The next step in our progression with ministry came when they invited us to join their small covenant group. This consists of three couples who meet once a month for a book review and dinner.

A great "vision" that was put into action and now serves many throughout our community.

Job Networking was not a very large concern for Georgia in 2004. However, as the housing and finance industry suffered, so suffered all industries and all employment in our state. As a couple, we looked for ways to get more involved in the church. Kathy became part of the New Member and Assimilation Committee. This ministry welcomes new members at a dinner for them. At one of these Spring dinners in 2008, the idea was circulated to host a dinner before the 7:00 p.m. Job Networking meetings for the Job Seekers. This was to be a dinner to provide nourishment and a spiritual message. The ministry was recruiting volunteers for the summer months to assist in setting up and serving the meals. Kathy has been with Job Networking ever since. She works with Mary Schaefer and Donna Litton. Together, they coordinate Table Hosts and assist any way they can.

John was recruited during that summer of 2008 to help as a Table Host. After hosting tables for a year and a half, Monday night table hosting has become a blessing. The people you meet at your table are the real reason for the ministry. And, their stories and experiences are amazing. At a Job Networking meeting after Christmas, one member of our table came to the conclusion that our table had enough talent to start our own business. This kind of comment was very well received by all of the people at the table. We often make jokes about who has the best table. But honestly, all the tables are the best. It is a tremendous opportunity and a joy to be able to be a Table Host.

We feel very blessed and humbled to be a part of RUMC Job Networking: a great "vision" that was put into action and now serves many throughout our community.

Kathy and John Glankler:

We have been members of RUMC since 2004. John is in construction finance and has worked across the United States. Kathy works part time for a tennis academy in Cobb County. We are members of the Bereans Sunday School Class, a couples' covenant group, and help with new member dinners. Kathy is a coordinator for Job Networking, and John is a Table Host. We were married in 1981. We have two children: Chelsea is a junior at the University of Dayton. Zachary, a graduate of Presbyterian College, is married and living in Austin, Texas.

Bill's Story

Reflections by a Table Leader and Dinner Speaker

My wife, Marilyn, and I have been members of Roswell United Methodist Church since 1982. Our whole family has been involved in most every program that the church has offered over those years: Youth, Sunday School, Bible Studies, service projects, missions, and many more. During the course of those early years we met Katherine and Craig Simons and have shared life together in the ensuing years.

One thing I learned in that relationship was that no one says "no" to Katherine! When RUMC first launched the dinners as an endeavor to provide a spiritual side to the Job Networking Ministry and I was approached to be a table leader, I wasn't about to say "no." In actuality, I was happy to do so. Three times during my thirty year career in the financial services industry (mostly the life insurance side), I had experienced unemployment. As with many of today's Job Seekers, I became a victim to downsizing and other economic belt-tightening measures. I never felt "fired," but the results were inevitably the same: no income, a wife and two kids to support and lots of monthly obligations. I knew I could be a good table leader. I wanted to be one. I understand the worries of the Job Seeker.

Fortunately, during all these difficult times of being without a job, I had various groups of Christian men with whom to share, to pray, and to network for new contacts. My weekly accountability group heard my frustrations and prayed regularly for my next interview. A breakfast men's group had so many people unemployed that they made an extra morning just for job networking and Bible study. Other professional friends and acquaintances helped me get in front of people that I didn't know. These efforts led to solid jobs all three times. I learned to "pray like it's all up to God, and work like it's all up to me." Most of all, each time I secured a new opportunity my faith was strengthened.

Faith is the first challenge, obstacle, or opportunity of unemployment. Can I trust God with my future? This question captures the essence of this challenge. At first blush the obvious answer is "yes!" Of course we can trust God. He is in control. He is trustworthy. He only has our best in mind. He knows better what we need than we do.

I learned to "pray like it's all up to God, and work like it's all up to me."

But shades of what if, what about, how can I, I can't, quickly conditioned my trust response. Many of us begin to evaluate the unknown future in light of the known past. How we feel about our past strongly affects our thinking about the future. In that subtle moment we shift our trust to our own ability and experience.

That shift can create a dual track in our mental processing. On one level, the spiritual, we still love and trust God. On the other, let's call it the practical level, we trust in our own strength, our perspective, our evaluation of the future. As a consequence, we develop an inner tension with questions we cannot easily answer. We want to completely trust our Lord, but don't we have to be practical? We want to be all out for God, but He certainly wants me to be responsible.

Can I trust God with my future? I learned that we should change the question. Can I trust God with His future? After all, who am I? I've been bought with a price. I'm a child of the King. I am his masterpiece, created to do the things he has already designed for me to do and equipped by Him to do exactly those things. He has promised to never leave me. There is nothing in his future that could possibly separate me from his love.

Because we cannot see the future we need to exercise faith. If we were not time-bound, faith would not be necessary. God does not need faith. He sees it all, past, present and future, in his eternal present. Because we cannot see clearly into our future we are uncertain as to which direction to go. Our great, incredible privilege is that the very God who created it all and sees it all is simply saying, "Trust me. I can see where your next step should be. I'll help you get there if you just trust me. Just have faith;" not faith in your abilities or past experiences; faith in the one who can see the next step, which He has carefully designed for you. Reminding and encouraging Job Seekers of this truth is my mission as I attend each meeting.

I'm sure that at a typical meeting of 300-400 Job Seekers there is a broad spectrum of people. For some, faith is barely on their radar screen. For others, they have been blessed to live a life of faith, before they became unemployed. Thus some will leave with different experiences from the spiritual side of the program. However, I do believe that all of them leave being reminded that they are not in this alone; that the warmth and love expressed by the volunteers is representative of the true presence and love of Jesus Christ. We're all special in His eyes, and that's a good thing to remember while you're down on yourself and on the world for being in this position.

As volunteers in the Job Networking Ministry it is indeed a privilege to be able to encourage and serve the Job Seekers. Of course, as with most things of this nature, one tends to get out of it more than one puts into it. I am continually amazed at the strength and faith of some of the people at my discussion table, many of whom have been out of work for a year or more. They truly inspire me. I also enjoy the fellowship of my fellow volunteers, many of whom I have known for years, while others are new friends.

At the end of each night I assure my table that I will be praying for them, but I also challenge them to come back...yes, for more networking...but, I want to see them back as a volunteer when they are successfully back to work. Many covenant to serve others as they have been served. It doesn't get much better than that!

Bill Goff:

I have been a member of RUMC since 1982. Both our son and daughter grew up in this church, and my wife and I have served on numerous boards and committees over the years. In 2003, I retired from a 30 year career in the insurance industry. Since that time I have used my consulting experience to help mission groups and ministries, do strategic planning, branding, and organizational effectiveness efforts. I also serve on the boards of several of these organizations. We have one grandson, who is two and a half years old.

Ernie's Story

The "Why am I Here"

I have been fortunate. Since I started working I have never been unemployed, and I have worked for the same company my entire career (although the company name has changed several times). However, I have been through more than a handful of downsizing "opportunities," both voluntary and involuntary. I strongly considered several of the voluntary opportunities and luckily avoided being tagged in the involuntary ones. So, I think I have some understanding of the anxiety, uncertainty and soul-searching that seem to go along with the realization that one has just lost a job or may soon experience that loss.

To decide between two options, I often visualize my situation in both scenarios: to try to get a feel of what my life would be like and what my feelings would be in one scenario versus the other. (That's why I never took advantage of the voluntary downsizing opportunities – I didn't like the way I thought I would feel without a job.) I empathize with those who unfortunately have to experience the reality of a life I only visualized. I prayed hard for guidance and wisdom each time the voluntary or involuntary downsizing ball rolled my way. I have also prayed for many work friends who were not as fortunate as I. Several have appeared at my job networking table. I ache when I see them struggle.

The "Okay, You Can Do This"

Several years ago when RUMC Job Networking was relatively young and being held exclusively in the church's youth building, I was considering a voluntary downsizing. I was curious to see how the program worked and to see what I could learn from it. That experience helped me visualize life without employment and as I said, I didn't like the image. After attending a couple of times I wanted to do something to help. So I started being a greeter, directing people to the right spots in the youth building. After a while one of the church staff asked if I would try being a "spiritual guide" (I think that was the term) by being on the lookout for Job Seekers who might need a caring ear – being available to listen to their emotional and spiritual concerns and direct them to the church staff if it appeared they needed more professional help. I was touched by some of the stories I heard.

Most of the time now, you will see me at Job Networking as a Table Host. That seemed to me to be an area where I could transfer some facilitation skills developed at work to a more sensitive and personal group discussion. I like the fact that we can talk about feelings and spiritual topics rather than just the process of how to get a job and that each person at the table has the opportunity to show care for and support to our other table partners. Hopefully, everyone leaves the table feeling a little better than before they sat down. I know I do.

Now, just because I am a Table Host doesn't mean that I am great at the role. There are others more competent as Table Hosts and others that are more consistent in their service. As with most of what I do at Job Networking, it doesn't come very naturally (it is work for me). But, I am willing to try. I try because I want to be receptive to God's call. I suspect that is what drives a lot of volunteers.

The "I Think I Can"

One of the areas that I see as strength of our Job Networking Ministry is the opportunity for Job Seekers to find a quiet time for individual prayer in the chapel. Obviously, we all need quiet time to talk with and listen to God, especially when we have so much trouble on our minds. This part of Job Networking calls for volunteers to be available to pray with these folks if they desire. We have several volunteers who are excellent prayer partners and this ability to pray with others seems to come naturally. In this area I am probably more the "think I can, think I can" steam engine than a sleek diesel. Never-the-less, I decided I should be one of those prayer volunteers, since I could use my Stephen Ministry training in this environment.

Once I turned it over totally to God and stopped meddling, God worked fast.

However, I underestimated the cold feet factor. The first time I volunteered to make myself available to pray one-to-one with Job Seekers in the chapel I sat on the back pew for a long time trying to talk God out of giving me that responsibility. I am not a "cold-call" salesman, so it was difficult to force myself to approach someone for such a personal matter. (I am still not totally comfortable with approaching someone and must admit that I am capable of talking myself out of it.) But that first night I kept getting the strong feeling that I needed to be with one particular gentleman, so I finally overcame my tentativeness and approached him. To my surprise he was receptive to allowing me to pray with him. I asked what we needed to pray about. I knew he would say, "Pray about my job loss" but was shocked when he told me the rest of his story – recent deaths in his family, possibility of divorce, a personal health issue, etc., in addition to the job concern. Turns out, the job loss was the least of his concerns. I felt crushed and depressed, just empathizing with him yet knowing I did not have to live through his pain. I am glad I followed God's urging and forced myself to approach this person. I trust God used that time to provide some measure of healing for him.

My point is that sometimes life comes to us in bunches and sometime those bunches are more thorns than rose petals. It is comforting to me to know that no matter what our situation, God cares. It is also comforting to know that He sends other people our way to help show His care. I have been the recipient of that care; I hope sometimes I can be the giver. That's why I try.

The "I Have to Appreciate God's Perspective"

Like most, life has come in bunches a couple of times for me too. In one year, my family experienced the birth of a child, terminal illness for my mother, heart attack for my father, lung cancer for my wife's mother, loss of her family's farm and fortune, loss of work for my wife's brother and the possibility of promotion to New York. I remember driving back and forth from Emory Hospital where my mother was, to Northside Hospital where my wife and newborn daughter were. (Talk about going from depths of depression to heights of joy; it was an emotional rollercoaster!)

We prayed a lot. We asked for God's deliverance, for wisdom, and for guidance on our decision whether to take the New York job. We wound up staying in Georgia to be close to our family. With God's help, it was one of my better life-choice decisions. During that year so many things happened that needed our close attention that could not have been given long distance, and we needed our church friends and support groups that we would have given up if we had moved. But mainly, during that time period I was able to be with my mother when she died. I could not have been there if we had moved north. While it may sound morbid, it was not. It was one of the most special, meaningful and religious experiences of my life – just she and I and God.

I would like to share one more story. When my son graduated from college, I prayed for him in his job search. As he worked through all the steps in pursuing a job, I prayed for specifics – for a particular interview to work, for a specific job to become available, etc. As a caring dad, I actually caused anxiety for myself by trying to "help" and by worrying over his job search efforts. Finally, I realized I was praying for the wrong thing – what I thought was right for him rather than what God thought was right for him. So, I changed my prayers to "God, I promise to stop trying to control this process; please guide him in the direction you want and place him in the job you think is best."

Amazingly, or maybe not amazingly, as soon as I began praying with a changed focus, things started happening quickly. On Monday, the interview that was scheduled for Tuesday got changed to Friday, because the interviewer had a family situation arise. On Tuesday, the company I was pushing as a good fit and secure job for him did in fact offer a job, but in a location he did not want. So, the company agreed to wait until the next month when openings would become available in the location he wanted. On Wednesday, another company my son had not even thought of pursuing called his cell phone to say they wanted to talk with him. On Thursday, he was offered that job. (Example of God's job networking: The supervisor received his resume from a former employee who had left that company to start his own business. The former employee was in a small group with a good Christian friend from my office, who in turn was impressed with my son's church activities.) So within less than a week God put all other doors on hold, while opening another door from "out of the blue." Once I turned it over totally to God and stopped meddling, God worked fast.

But that's only half of the story. I didn't mention earlier that I had also been praying, since he was a boy, that my son would find the kind of wife that God intended for him. So, the "rest of the story" is that as a direct result of that job, my son met someone who would become his future wife! While I was focused on things like job benefits and security, God was focused on relationships. God's perspective was so much greater than mine (duh!) p.s. had my son accepted the other offer, he would have been laid off by now. He certainly would not have found the person God selected for him to marry. I just have to keep reminding myself that God deals in relationships and that His perspective is always based on love. I believe that is the basis of His job networking.

Ernie Bond:

I am a volunteer Table Host and prayer partner for Job Networking. I have been a member of RUMC since 1977 where I am in the Berea's Sunday school and Stephen Ministry. I am married to Linda (36 years) and we have two grown married children and one grandson. I have been employed 40 years in the telecommunications industry, basically with the same company (although the company names have changed from divestitures and mergers.) I enjoy sports, time with family and friends, and playing with my grandson.

Jeanne's Story

Praying for Our Neighbor in Need

6:45 p.m. Soft instrumental sounds fade as four prayer partners approach the Chapel's altar to seek the Lord.

"Create in me a clean heart, O Lord, and renew a right spirit within me."

"Come, Holy Spirit, and pray for us. We do not know how to pray for these Job Seekers, but you do."

7:00 p.m. Men and women Job Seekers and a few other prayer partners make their way into the chapel. The room is soon abuzz with whispered conversation and prayer.

Some sit alone in quiet supplication. Others group together in threes. Most people are teamed with a prayer partner.

I've been part of the prayer ministry at my church for many years and regularly pray for Job Seekers' requests when I see them on the prayer lists. When asked to organize a time for prayer at Job Networking, I willingly agreed. We quickly found that most people want to share and pray with one individual.

I approach a person and ask, "Would you like someone to pray with you?" If they agree, I sit down beside them and listen as the person paints a verbal picture regarding a previous job situation, family, job searching, whatever they wish to reveal. I know that the Lord is near to the brokenhearted. I depend upon the Lord to guide my prayers in accordance with His will and for the good of the Seeker.

My trust level has increased. The first few times I prayed with an unknown Job Seeker, even though I had prayed for guidance and had come equipped with several scriptures to pray that seemed pertinent, I was uneasy. But God has demonstrated Romans 8:26-28 over and over. "And the Holy Spirit helps us in our weakness." For example, we don't know what God wants us to pray for. But the Holy Spirit prays for us with groaning that cannot be expressed in words. And the Father who knows all hearts knows what the Spirit is saying, for the Spirit pleads for us believers in harmony with God's own will. "And we know that God causes everything to work together for the good of those who love God and are called according to his purpose for them."

I know that the Lord is near to the brokenhearted.

I believe that God hears the prayers of His people. I believe that God loves each person. When we come together seeking Him, He is there. My fellow prayer partners and I have discovered that we love this time of prayer. We don't want to miss it. What a privilege to go to God with someone, to be in His presence together! He guides our praying and touches the men and women. I am so grateful to God and to the Job Seekers for letting me pray with them.

Our prayer partners do not assume that a Job Seeker is a Christian, though most of the people who come for prayer have a Christian background. However, some people have been away from God and church for years. Their job search and prayer time are an opportunity to seek and renew. One of my friends had the special privilege of praying with someone to receive Christ as Savior.

We've seen a number of occasions where God's hand must have selected the right prayer partner for the Job Seeker. How rewarding it is when that happens. We've seen many tense faces relax during prayer. Sometimes, they just sit in the peace of the Spirit as we move to the next person.

Our prayer partners display different styles and different gifts. So do the people who receive. I am very glad to be one part of this ministry.

Jeanne Motley:

I am a Prayer Partner for the RUMC Job Networking Ministry and a member of RUMC since 1988. I am a musician and have taught in the public school system. I play C Flute and Bass flute with the Atlanta Flute Ensemble and the Alpharetta City Band. My family's business is in the mortgage industry.

Ruthie's Story

Ruthie Powell and "The Ruthie List – How it Works...and...Common Mistakes Made by Job Seekers"

I have been a Recruiter "since before the earth cooled"! I have served in all levels of Human Resources capacities, and have also recruited on the agency side for over 20 years. I have worked in virtually every vertical industry area of recruiting. This wealth of experience has helped me to have a broad range of knowledge about many aspects of corporate America and "what they are looking for" in the candidates they consider for their position openings.

Although I recruit for a living, I guess I am most "famous" for "The Ruthie List!" The Ruthie List is a 12 year old list of OVER 8,000 members, made up of ONLY Recruiters and Human Resources professionals working primarily in Atlanta, Georgia, who are interested in helping one another. My belief is that the true meaning of life is "You can get anything in life you want if you'll just help enough other people get what they want."

The FREE list is used to post open positions (encouraging referrals) and to post available candidates (encouraging referrals) and to keep the HR/recruiting community informed about professional meetings, etc.

Like most folks, I have lost jobs in the past. In 2002, the only thing Atlanta technical companies needed less than a Computer Programmer was a recruiter to find one!

I began attending the Job Seeker meetings at Fuddruckers in the 1990's.

There is a new level of fear and hopelessness this time, even more so than 1981, 1991 and after September 11.

I just showed up and helped anyone I could. As a recruiter with solid human resources knowledge and experience, I could always find ways to help direct/connect people. When email "was invented/became the norm" I just started forwarding everyone's job openings to everyone I knew, and people started getting jobs!

As a Job Seeker, I learned that the more people who know about a candidate's availability and the more people who know about a job opening, the more likely to make a match.

In recent times, I have noticed there are a greater number of older candidates, many of whom have been laid off for the first time, and many after 30+ years of work with the same employer.

There is a new level of fear and hopelessness this time, even more so than 1981, 1991 and after September 11, 2001 which impacted 2002.

I love sharing my life-long experiences (which have taught me well) with others who are struggling. One of my quotes is "Anything is easy when you know how…even brain surgery to a brain surgeon." That's why it seems so hard to get a job. People don't know how! Things that are second nature to me are unfortunately very foreign to the typical Job Seeker. Whenever I have given my speech, Job Seekers come to me afterward and say "Why hasn't anyone told us these things before?" I am assured that my message has been a help to those in attendance.

It is not unusual for me to hear back from unemployed attendees that as soon as they posted their "new resume" and followed the subject line and email format I recommended, they immediately started getting interviews!

Without exception, as I work with Job Seekers at RUMC, there is a gratitude, appreciation and kindness from the Job Seeker. They are so thankful for direction, advice and helpful information. It truly warms my heart to be able to make a difference in their lives

I not only enthusiastically tell others about the Job Networking meetings, throughout Atlanta, but on a weekly basis I send emails to all the Job Networking yahoo groups. I also send the announcement to all 8000 members of TheRuthieList group. I have a template email which tells about all the job network meetings in the Atlanta Metro area. These include:

AFUMCCareerResources@yahoogroups.com

Atlanta_job_search@yahoogroups.com;

atlantabusinesslinks@yahoogroups.com

careermavens@yahoogroups.com;

jobseekersrevenge@yahoogroups.com;

RUMCjobnet@yahoogroups.com;

refocusoncareers@yahoogroups.com;

decaturseekers@yahoogroups.com

JFBCJobNet@yahoogroups.com

JCUMC_Job_Network@yahoogroups.com

careerquest_sa@yahoogroups.com

C3G_WednesdayWomen@yahoogroups.com

aleventhal@jfcs-atlanta.org

amccollum@cascadeumc.org

jobs@fbcw.net

rmawn@st-ann.org

hcasey@mustministries.org

jean@careerministry.org

bray@mustministries.org

kettering.ruthie@gmail.com

Job Seekers in Atlanta are very fortunate to have the many networking opportunities offered. RUMC has an excellent program with professionalism and infrastructure. However, the Job Seekers group at Perimeter Mall area on Friday mornings is well run and helps many. The newer but highly effective "C3G" groups are actually helping a lot of Job Seekers with the leadership of only a few.

Today at Job Networking, I volunteer as a Table Host, Resume Reviewer and Speaker. I am basically a shy person (I give speeches, but I am uncomfortable walking up to others and introducing myself). I believe that the people who come are very intimidated, and I learned to be warm and even humorous to put them at ease.

Years ago my husband lost his job and I took him to a Job Seekers meeting, and as we went into the building he said, "I feel like I'm going to the dentist to have my teeth drilled." From that, I never forget how "scary" this all can be to the Job Seeker.

Some harsh realities that have to be faced in this work are:

- If you're not getting interviews/offers you're doing it wrong;
- Getting a job is a job and you have to work at it all day every day;
- You can't get a job sitting at home – you MUST be willing to meet others;
- You can get anything in life you want, if you'll just help enough other people get what they want;
- You can't afford to feel sorry for yourself;
- Everything in life happens for a reason, and it is not our place to question why;

Words of Advice:

- To someone thinking about volunteering in such a program, just volunteer one time, and you'll be hooked for life!
- To a church or organization considering starting such a ministry, look at how RUMC does it and duplicate it. Apply the areas where you sense the need and have the volunteers. But, whatever you choose to do, do it well."
- To a Job Seeker; attending job network meetings is the ONLY way to effectively get a job...any other system will not compare to the results of these ministries.

I truly enjoy being part of this group of volunteers because they are the very embodiment of Christians who freely give of their time to help others.

Ruthie Powell:

I am the Founder of The Ruthie List and volunteer speaker to Job Seeker groups throughout Atlanta. I have served in all levels of Human Resources capacities, and have also recruited on the agency side for over 20 years, specializing in technical/IT recruiting. I graduated from Mississippi State University in Business, and have since worked in virtually every vertical industry area of recruiting (all levels of insurance, IT/technical, legal, accounting/finance, and sales/marketing. I currently serve as Senior Recruiter for Travelers Insurance.

Richard's Story

My career experiences prior to Job Seeker volunteer work

My first experience being unemployed occurred in 1999. In the previous 28 years of my career, I had successfully changed occupations and employers "at will" in order to improve my management capabilities and income. I had chosen to change management roles that took me from engineering to HR to marketing and ultimately to sales. During this time in my career, I chose to switch employers six times which included working for a Fortune 100 firm, a pre-IPO venture capital funded startup, and other intermediate sized companies. The 1999 job market was very strong and when I first became unemployed at that time, I was confident that I could find a job that was equal to or better than my last one. I was right. In short order, I landed an interim job. I continued to seek something better, did not stop networking, and landed a great job at 50% more salary within the next six months.

It starts because you desire to give back to others and help them during a time of need.

My second experience being involuntarily unemployed occurred in 2001. During this period, the job market was weak. I was less confident I could find another desirable position quickly. For this reason, I started attending church Job Seeker meetings and professional/industry group meetings to (a) expand my networking contacts and (b) learn new strategies for a job search. This was my first experience with church Job Seeker meetings and I found them to be highly variable in terms of usefulness for me. The most helpful part of church Job Seeker programs (for me), were the speakers who were experts in job seeking strategies. The least helpful parts of these programs were the attempts to facilitate participants "networking" with each other. (To this day, my opinions have not changed.)

After attending Job Seeker and professional meetings for about six months, I assessed the current 2001 job market and the state of my industry: telecommunications. I concluded that finding a job in a timely manner would be very difficult and that the prospects for attaining my former income were low. I decided I was ready for another major change in my career. After considerable contemplation, I decided to become trained in the career coaching profession (my 5th occupation!) and start my own career coaching firm.

My early Job Seeker volunteer work

My volunteer experiences with Job Seekers began in early 2002, when I first started guest speaking for several church Job Seeker groups in North Atlanta. This was during the downturn that followed 9/11/2001 and the subsequent lukewarm jobs recovery. I began this volunteer work because I recognized that there were a great number of people who needed to increase their job search knowledge through such groups and because I felt a trained career coach could add to the information provided by the lay leaders.

After speaking to a wide range of church Job Seeker groups of many denominations for several years, I decided in 2006 to become involved on a regular basis. Since I was familiar with the RUMC Job Networking Ministry and knew that the program was growing, I chose to become a consistent volunteer with them. My first duties involved reviewing resumes of Job Seekers. When the leadership decided to expand the program into additional services, I asked to run a job interview session that would give seekers a chance to learn expert strategies to be more effective in their interviews. Thus, The Interview Room was born in 2007.

The Interview Room and other volunteer work

Since 2007, I have continued to volunteer as the leader of The Interview Room. Because I believe in the overall mission of the ministry, I am given the freedom to control the content that I present. Moreover, the program leaders are great people with whom to work. These are the keys to retaining someone like me as a long-term volunteer.

In addition to The Interview Room, I have volunteered for the past three years as an Industry Guide for the HR profession. This provides me an opportunity to interact with a manageable number of Job Seekers on an individual basis. In addition, I have also continued to speak as a guest on job search strategies for a considerable variety of other church Job Seeker groups in North Atlanta. I regularly receive positive comments from attendees at all my events. As long as I feel I am making a positive contribution that is appreciated, I intend to continue with all these activities.

Specific to The Interview Room, my basic approach to interview coaching in a group environment is to provide a handout at each meeting. This provides a structure for interaction with the group, insuring that all attendees are provided with a baseline of knowledge that most participants need. Beyond this, time is normally left for questions and answers from the attendees. This provides the ability for people with specific questions to become informed and receive some personal attention to their needs. When additional time is available, there are options for interactive role plays with attendees. I hope in the future to be able to show videos that provide interview examples. I am developing such DVDs as part of my career coaching program materials.

To recap, the materials/information options currently being used (or planned for use) in The Interview Room are:

- A "basic knowledge" handout provided in every session to all attendees and reviewed by the group leader;
- A freeform question and answer segment that allows for individualized topics;
- Optional time for interactive role plays. These are directed by the group leader in which the leader may choose to take the role of the interviewer or the interviewee, based upon what will be most effective at that time;
- If available and time permits, videos or other support materials may be added.

I believe the critical factors that other program leaders would want to consider in developing an interview coaching program of their own are:

- A decision must be made to make the program a group event led by an individual or to create a more personalized, one-to-one program. The latter option requires much more expert resources per Job Seeker. I know of at least one church that has a small number of seekers and quite a few volunteers, making the one-to-one format more practical. For larger programs, I believe this is not practical when a quality program is desired;
- Careful selection is necessary to find a group leader who is a true expert in job interviewing. I have found that many church Job Seeker groups allow minimally qualified people to run their programs and the programs lack quality. Often recruiters and HR professionals are generically viewed as experts in job search areas, although this is not necessarily true. The leader must be outgoing, friendly, non-judgmental, and encouraging in order to create a nurturing environment;
- The leader's selection of content and media to be provided is critical to the learning process. All presentations need to be professionally prepared and conducted;

- The choice of facilities in which the program will be held is important for conducting an effective group session. The room must be free from outside noise distractions and for workshops where practice interview coaching sessions are to be conducted, extra space for small group breakouts will be needed;
- The interview coaching program must fit with the overall Job Seeker meeting schedule. Our Interview Room runs concurrently (in parallel) with other such "breakout" sessions, and it is critical that the program follows a tight time schedule, so that Job Seekers can participate in other program activities.

Over the past years while facilitating The Interview Room, I have seen a shift in attendee demographics toward more over-45 Job Seekers. I believe this reflects the general population in the white-collar unemployed segment in suburban Atlanta. I imagine other programs located in more ethnically diverse sections of town would see more diversity in their participants. Most attendees appear, like the general population, to lack job search skills and gain considerable benefits from the program. After every session several participants come and thank me personally, which is my most direct feedback as to the value they perceive from them.

General suggestions regarding church Job Seeker groups

As mentioned earlier, a major factor in developing a group of volunteers for a church Job Seeker ministry is the style of the leaders. The leaders set the tone for the group, which will have a huge influence on attracting and retaining program volunteers. Leaders need to define the program scopes clearly, and then actively pursue expert volunteer resources.

In addition to the careful selection of Leaders, there needs to be a consistent mechanism for volunteer and Job Seeker feedback. The simplest way to do this is via feedback forms. Job Seeker programs (especially new ones) can provide a brief feedback questionnaire to their participants asking them to identify which parts of the program were of benefit and what else they would like to see provided.

For someone considering volunteering in a Job Seeker program, it starts because you desire to give back to others and help them during a time of need. It is important to consider whether you have a critical expertise that is needed. However there are many roles and most programs have a shortage of expertise in narrow areas such as interviewing, networking, resumes, etc. Volunteer where you can be of most help.

To a church or organization considering starting a ministry, I encourage significant consideration, before launching a new group. Identify all the existing similar groups in your area of town and make a reasoned decision as to how your new group will provide value to Job Seekers in your community and to your congregation.

Richard Kirby:

I can be reached at (678) 547-0072 or at rkirby@executive-impact.com. My career services web site is www.executive-impact.com. My job search book, *Fast Track Your Job Search (and Career!)*, is available at www.fasttrackyourjobsearch.com.

Bill's Story

Workshop title: Entrepreneurship for the Corporate Soul

I first started with the RUMC Job Networking Ministry volunteering in the resume review efforts and chairing one of the quarterly roundtables entitled Start a Business. My work in outplacement as a career counselor had allowed me to review and modify hundreds of resumes and it was obvious there were many Job Seekers who were in need of help.

There are, simply put, a lot of really poor resumes out there and a resume is a marketing document. A resume must represent the individual in the best possible manner. I was also asked to become an Industry Guide for "wanna be" entrepreneurs and I have had the pleasure of speaking to quite a few people who have an interest in starting or acquiring a business of their own.

As the economy worsened in the latter half of 2008, the flow of Job Seekers into the RUMC Job Networking Ministry continued to increase. It became apparent that the seekers needed additional resources added to the current offerings. I volunteered to lead a short workshop on small business start up or entrepreneurship. With the able assistance of Don Schuster and Joe Judge, we launched our presentation. We now offer a high level briefing on Starting a Business, Buying a Business and Home Based Choices along with handouts to help find additional resources. In the time available, we can only present the bare bones but our audience has continued to grow from a handful to sometimes as many as 25-30 interested potential entrepreneurs. It became obvious to me that even more information was needed so we began to offer a full 2 hour workshop, primarily focused on how to evaluate franchise opportunities.

We now offer the "briefing" on "Starting a Business, Buying a Business and Home Based Choices" twice per month, as well as the more complete workshop, "Steps to Owning a Franchise" twice each month. Every session is presented in an educational format without any personal interests or promotion of materials and services. We occasionally must discourage aggressive audience members, who may want to promote their particular business interests, so as to not allow our Job Seekers to become compromised by confrontational opportunists. We do our best to keep our motivations and content pure.

Why do I continue to volunteer? Offering the knowledge I have gained through my consulting services to those in need through the workshop format has certainly lead to network connections that have been positive for my business. Equally, I learned during my last job search that I enjoy helping others. If I can assist someone in preventing a poor decision or help them in making a good decision, I have contributed to providing a path to a new beginning.

Statistics tell us that at least 70% of all employed adults in the U.S. dream about working for themselves, to "some day" start a business of their own. The same statistics tell us that approximately two out of 100, actually follow through. During my last job change, I recognized that I was one of those 70%, but I had never done anything about it. Out of fear, lack of knowledge and wrong perception, as yet, I had failed to act. Now, my mission is to find others like myself. I know they are out there, holding back, fearful of change, fearful of failure, fearful of financial ruin and fearful of being sold something they don't want. My desire is to help those individuals become informed, to guide them on how to make the best possible decision for their families and their own future. Their best choice may be to regain employment, but at least they make the decision based upon facts and with confidence.

As I write this, in the past year I have had two individuals listen to our "Start a Business" briefing that became clients and successfully chose to become new franchise owners. One of these individuals has become a colleague in my business organization. We contributed to finding a new career direction for both. Of course, their journeys are still in progress, but the steps already taken clearly have demonstrated success for both.

Seeing a spark in their eyes, a lighter step in their walk, and a hint of hope in their voices is exciting and fulfilling.

The Job Seekers have changed over the past three years, more numerous to be sure. We are seeing an older segment, more people over 50, many in senior "C" level roles, pushed out of corporate employment. Many have little chance of gaining re-employment without moving to another part of the country, taking a considerable cut in compensation or taking a position not reflective of their capabilities and past accomplishments. Facts are facts and age discrimination is real. The harsh reality is that for many people in this category, their best choice is a complete change in career direction, sometimes into business ownership.

Once a month, I travel to the greater Houston area, at the invitation of a colleague and present a workshop about franchising at their Between Jobs Ministry. The BJM, as it's commonly referred to, is a bit larger than the program offered by RUMC and is staffed by mostly retired, nearly full time volunteers. The BJM program is offered every week, on Wednesday mornings and is at least a half day curriculum of workshops and seminars along the same theme as those offered by RUMC. There appears to be more one-to-one counseling available for those more distraught Job Seekers, but the intent is consistent. They offer a variety of job/career assistance programs; from resume review, interviewing tips, networking advice, compensation negotiations, career change, to business ownership. Yes, BJM is also a career ministry first and foremost. It is open to all faiths without hesitation and offering hope and encouragement along with very much needed information.

I believe in what I'm doing as a volunteer. I acknowledge that my business can benefit from my efforts. I also recognize that providing information, offering a small word of encouragement, directing them to other resources, while providing consulting and coaching without cost or obligation helps people make changes in their lives and careers. Seeing a spark in their eyes, a lighter step in their walk, and a hint of hope in their voices is exciting and fulfilling on its own. And that's why I continue to be a volunteer.

Bill Williams:

I have 25+ years in a variety of senior executive positions in technology companies. I am a former Army officer and have been self employed for the past 9 years as an executive recruiter, career consultant for a major outplacement firm, certified business coach and business owner. After all this time, I finally found my perfect business and immensely enjoy my current role in franchise and business brokerage: helping people make good choices when deciding to become business owners themselves.

Tim's Story

About That Resume

In 2004, I joined Write Choice Services for the express purpose of continuing the resume writing portion of the business. A friend, who was a business coach and led a weekly JAWS (job accountability weekly schedule) group for Job Seekers, approached me and asked if I would participate in his group and review the resumes of the Job Seekers who attended. One week, my friend encouraged me to "branch out" and to attend RUMC Job Networking to see if my services could be used there as well. I went and I asked if another resume reviewer would be welcome. I've been helping out ever since.

In my nearly six years as a volunteer, I have also been the "featured speaker" on two occasions. I am one of the "Ask an Expert" roundtable leaders and an Industry Guide. My regular responsibility is leading a workshop on writing a resume.

When attendance at the meetings ballooned to more than 300 Job Seekers, the good folks reviewing resumes were hard pressed to see everyone who sought a one-to-one review. Even with 30 or more reviewers working for 75 minutes or longer, some Job Seekers still waited in line when the formal meeting began. I offered to design and to lead a resume writing workshop during the resume review time. Perhaps having a workshop as an option would help ease the burden for the reviewers.

Now Job Seekers have an option of waiting in line to get a one-to-one review or attending the resume review workshop where they can "self-critique" and ask questions. The workshop consistently attracts at least 15 participants and sometimes as many as 30 have crowded into the session. The workshop is also a resource for the resume reviewers. If they feel stymied by a Job Seeker's resume, the reviewer can suggest that the Job Seeker attend the workshop and/or seek me out to address a particular issue.

A little entertainment and a bit of laughter go a long way.

I have worked for two different resume writing companies, have attended professional resume writers' conferences and do my best to keep current with concepts and ideas around resume content and format. I strive to offer what I believe is the "best of the best." I present the format that I personally use and I explain why. I tell the Job Seekers that there are other resume writers who use different formats and would actually do some things completely opposite to what I do. That is fine. I know that what I do works for my clients. The Job Seekers' responsibility is to determine for him or herself what will work best for them.

Here are some of the basics that we teach:

- If you have worked for at least 5 years, then you should generate a two page resume, not 1 ¼ or 1 ½ or 1 and a little bit more;
- A one page resume is satisfactory, but I don't recommend it;
- Two pages is the maximum length, unless the Job Seeker is an executive;
- A resume needs only go back 10 years;
- The resume should clearly indicate that the Job Seeker is qualified for the position for which the resume has been submitted. If the recruiter or HR person has to determine how an individual is qualified, most likely the resume will be discarded;

- The Job Seeker may need to modify the resume each time it is submitted, so that it speaks directly to the job opening;
- For each job that one has held, provide a short job description, then list bullet points showing the impact one has had on that job (far too many resumes simply bullet point one's job description and give no indication of what impact the individual had on the job);
- Use adjectives – don't just be an engineer or a teacher or a dog catcher. Be outstanding, superb, top notch, exceedingly competent and use the strongest adjective that you feel is reasonable;
- Use action verbs – drove, spearheaded, engineered, generated, built from the ground up. Overuse of words like designed, developed, implemented, etc., quickly becomes monotonous;
- Do not worry about a work history that may look "sketchy." Provide the job description and generate at least 2 solid bullet points of impact. If you can show that you had an impact on a company in a part time or in a short term contract position, imagine what that suggests you could do if you had a full time, ongoing job with a company – Wow! What an impact you could have then.
- If you have international work or study experience (not just foreign travel) this needs to be highlighted;
- Look at your email address – does it suggest something that you don't want it to suggest about you, especially in a job search? If so, get a new account for the job search;
- If you have been promoted while working for a company, make that a bullet point. Don't assume that the hiring person will see a change in title as a promotion; it might only be seen as a lateral move;

- If you have earned a degree, spell it out e.g. **BACHELOR OF ARTS DEGREE IN MATHMATICS.** Let there be no doubt that you earned it;
- List computer skills, especially if you are of the baby boomer generation (I am and we are not always thought to know these things);
- Always include a cover letter.

Although I am firm with my resume writing style and the guidelines I present, I am quick to add and I repeat throughout the workshop, "Ultimately, you have to be comfortable with the document and its format. Do what makes sense for you."

I have fun leading the workshop. Laughter breaks out frequently, usually at my expense. A little entertainment and a bit of laughter go a long way is easing the burden of the job seeking journey.

By the way, I am not a member of RUMC and I was a United Church of Christ pastor. Why do I volunteer? Because it is a ministry in which lives are touched and impacted. I see a spark of hope come into eyes that have been listless, as an individual discovers some way to improve his or her resume, job search, and networking. When 15, 20 even 30 people gather in the workshop room, they suddenly realize they truly are not alone in trying to improve their resume. I watch as these Job Seekers speak to one another, encourage one another, and even laugh together. And I see the beginning of healing occur in lives filled with pain.

I volunteer because I am fed as well through the camaraderie of the volunteers. It is an honor and a blessing to be a part of such an amazing group of people.

Dr. Tim Morrison:

In a major career shift of my own, I left ministry after 25 years, tried a couple of different occupations and then joined Write Choice Services, Inc. I bought the company when the founder/owner retired. I am a published author of books and articles, an editor and writing coach. I have lived in seven states as well as in Ghana, West Africa. My wife, Marta, and I reside in Marietta, Georgia.

I can be reached at: tim@writechoiceservices.com.

Gary's Story

Job Networking Dinner

My name is Gary Grant and I have been a member of RUMC since 1988. When Katherine first suggested the Table Host concept for the dinner portion of Job Networking and asked if I would participate, I thought it would be a great idea. In the past three years, prior to the start of dinner at Job Networking I have served as table discussion leader at Souly Business men's retreats and a discussion leader for Men Step Up Friday morning lay Christian Bible study. The concept of discussing key points of the dinner speaker's topic enables table participants to dive into the message and internalize it for their current circumstances. I have served with Job Networking as a Table Host since the first time we started to have dinner and discussions prior to the start of the "real" program of Job Networking Sessions. At first I struggled with being the host at the table as there is a wide diversity of involvement during the discussions from the participants. I was unable to bond with the participants in such a short time. I finally found my comfort zone by focusing on listening and not on problem solving. I could not get jobs for the people at my table, but I could let them know I cared about them, loved them and would pray for them.

After I had served as a Table Host for about three months, I was asked to be the dinner speaker. I could not get my arms around my talk topic and then I realized that I could address a true story about Jesus and His redemption through his resurrection and how He came back so He could live in us to live through us.

This is the story and it is a story about:

Human Failure

A Woman of faith

Her marriage commitment

Her continuous prayer

Answered Prayer

God's Grace

God's Love

God's forgiveness

God's relentless pursuit of Union

Human Failure

My character is Joe; I have changed his real name to protect his identity. Joe struggled in life trying to over achieve. He never felt good enough or accepted. He started his life with club feet. After years of casts and surgery, his legs and feet were repaired, but he maintained a competitive struggle with a twin brother who did not have any handicap.

The competition came early in his life. Joe never wanted to be second. In school he studied harder than anyone. He earned his Eagle Scout rank. In sports, he excelled in baseball and football until two knee injuries ended his football career. He became class President in high school and was voted "most likely to succeed" in the Senior Year Book.

In college Joe was elected to student senate, served as house Treasurer in his fraternity and walked on the baseball team in his freshman year. He met his future wife on a blind date his freshman year and their three year romance ended in marriage the week after they graduated from college. The year was 1970 and jobs were hard to find. Joe and his wife went back to school and moved into married housing. Joe worked odd jobs while she taught school. All the while they worked on their Master's degrees. Joe's wife noticed a recurring theme. Joe would get home late from work and have a few drinks. Joe didn't seem happy. They went to a college counselor and he told them the pitfalls of marriage. Life became a struggle. Having been an ROTC student in college, Joe was given a medical discharge as he was getting ready to become a 2nd Lt. in the Army. Too many knee injuries and his club feet kept him out. His Achilles tendons no longer stretched. He could not stand at attention for very long before he fell over. The drinking continued and an occasional party with pot. Normal for the decade, she thought.

When they graduated with their Masters degrees, they moved to Atlanta. She became a full time high school teacher earning $12,500 a year. Joe was a computer technician, earning $4,500 a year. Once again, he felt like a failure. Joe's drinking became a daily event. He came home late and usually drunk. Joe thought it was a normal male characteristic. Work hard, drink hard. After two years of marriage, Joe left to find himself! Joe was not happy and he believed the marriage was going nowhere.

After 4 months of separation, Joe and his wife tried to reconcile. During the reconciliation, Joe's wife became pregnant. They could not live on Joe's $4,500 a year salary. Joe found a new job in Dayton, OH. They moved to Dayton and Joe's wife thought this would be a fresh start for the three of them.

Joe worked in Dayton for about a year and was transferred to Waterloo, Canada. Not wanting to move his family there, he commuted every other week. After six months, Joe was transferred to New York City. Again, Joe did not move his family. His wife was now pregnant with their second child. Joe commuted to New York City every week.

Joe thought this was a great life. He had a two-story brownstone in Greenwich Village, where he lived during the week and a wife and two children in Dayton, where he spent the weekends.

AWESOME! No one questioned what he did. During the week, Joe partied every night, never getting home until 2am or later. On weekends, Joe flew home to Dayton to be a husband and dad for two days then back to the party city.

Joe's drinking was becoming a real problem. Even worse, drugs entered the picture. Realizing that he was either going to lose his family or die from his exploits in NYC, Joe asked for a transfer to Indianapolis.

With the transfer granted, Joe moved his wife and two children with the third on the way to Indy. With good intentions, Joe took a job where he was home every night. Well almost. Joe joined a country club and that became the substitute for his New York City life and activities. Now there was a combination of drinking, drugs, golf and gambling.

A Woman of Faith

The only difference from all the other cities where they lived was Joe's wife joined the church. Not Joe…who needed God? Joe's wife needed something to grab hold of. She worked to make ends meet as most of the family's discretionary income went to golf, drinking and gambling. She was raising their three children on her own, as Joe took little interest. The children feared their dad. Fear engulfed his wife as well. There was no physical abuse but the worst kind of abuse - verbal. Physical wounds eventually heal, but wounds of the heart last forever.

In order to save their marriage, she took a bold step. At the suggestion of her pastor she insisted they attend a United Methodist Marriage Encounter weekend. Joe realized he had better go or would risk losing everything. Joe was touched and he invited Christ into his life. Joe's wife believed that finally her prayers were answered. Unfortunately, Joe's drinking sabbatical lasted only two years and when he resumed drinking, Joe did so with vengeance.

Joe moved his family three more times from 1981 to 1987: from Indianapolis to Bradenton, Fl., next to Sarasota, Fl. and finally a stop in Tampa, Fl. During those years Joe's wife continued to pray for God's intervention. Each day she looked for a sign to strengthen her. Joe's drinking and late night adventures continued.

Filled with remorse after a night on the town, Joe stopped at a friend's house to confess his transgressions. At his friend's insistence Joe agreed to attend his first AA meeting. Joe invited his wife to go along as it was an open meeting where anyone could attend. His wife was ready to go to support her husband at the AA meeting. For her there was a glimmer of hope. Would God now answer her prayer?

At the end of the AA meeting they went back to the car together. They sat in silence for a minute. Then Joe said, "Those people are alcoholics; they need help. I am not like them! I am not an alcoholic and I don't need this!"

Joe's wife was once again devastated.

Another two years passed. Again after a night on the town, Joe realized he had a problem. He had gone to his doctor who saw that his vital signs showed issues from drinking. Joe's physician recommended a therapist for counseling instead of AA. In Joe's own mind he thought he drank because of stress at work and his poor relationship with his wife.

At the end of the first session, the therapist told Joe, "I would drink also, if I was married to a wife like yours."

That's all Joe needed. He immediately went home told his wife what the therapist had said! He drank because of her! It was her problem! She had to change, not him. Totally devastated she ran to her closet, closed the door and sobbed as she prayed to God….WHY!

Once again they moved. Joe had changed companies. This time it was back to Atlanta in 1988. Their children were now in the 8th, 6th and 4th grades. Joe's drinking continued taking a heavy toll on the family. Relations were strained. The children dreaded to hear their father's footsteps when he came home from work. They knew he would go straight for the bottle.

God's Grace, Intervention, and Perfect Timing

Three years had gone by since their move to Atlanta. Joe's drinking and recreational drug use continued. Toward the end of 1991 Joe was seeing Essey, a Jewish hypnotist for sessions to quit smoking. By the end of February 1992, it was clear to Essey that there was a bigger issue than Joe's need to quit smoking. Essey told Joe that during his hypnotic sessions there was guilt, remorse and loathing of himself over his drinking. He hated what he was doing to his family and himself and the first issue to get under control was his drinking. Joe trusted Essey and realized she was right. The embarrassing moments were more frequent and his behavior needed to change.

What he does promise is that He will always be with me.

Essey sent Joe to Dr. Gordon, a counselor, who specialized in therapy. By the end of his third session, Dr. Gordon told Joe, "I can continue to take your money, but I am never going to be able to solve your problem. If you have a heart problem you need to see a heart specialist. You have a drinking problem and you need to see a drinking specialist. You need to go to AA! Here is their address and if you leave now you can make the 10:30 a.m. meeting!"

Broken, ashamed and reaching for help, Joe went to that AA meeting at 10:30 am March 4, 1992. March 5 was his wife's birthday. That evening they went out to dinner. As they sat down they ordered drinks. His wife ordered water. Joe ordered iced tea.

His wife looked puzzled. "No Scotch? What's going on? Are you sick?"

"Yes, actually, I am. I am an alcoholic and for your birthday present I am attending AA to get help."

Joe's words shocked his wife. She was afraid to believe, after so many let downs. Yet she wanted to believe. In her mind, she silently hoped that after 22 years of praying for Joe, for their marriage, for Joe to quit his chemical dependency that the healing had arrived.

On March 4, 2010, Joe will celebrate18 years of sobriety. Much has happened in those 18 years. God worked through a Jewish hypnotist to get Joe's attention and led him out of darkness. Because of God's relentless pursuit Joe met Jesus face to face behind those closed doors at AA. On March 4, 1992 Joe started the first day of the rest of his life. Joe's wife and children celebrate March 4 with the joy and spirit of new birth: a party with cake, candles and ice cream even to this day… It is a red letter day.

If you don't mind I would like to introduce you to Joe's wife. She sits in front of me, a Table Host at table #2. I have watched her all night during my talk. I am sure she relives the hard times, but she is grateful for God's grace, faithfulness and answered prayer. I also am sure that she has been praying for me this entire evening. I would like to introduce you to Gwen Grant, my lovely wife and my soul mate and gift from God. You see Joe's real name is Gary! This has been Gwen's and Gary's story. But really it is God's story.

During the last 18 years, we have renewed our marriage vows twice. Our first renewal was February 14, 1993 during a marriage renewal weekend sponsored by RUMC. I can picture the moment as if it were yesterday. We sat cross legged Indian style, facing each other: my legs wrapped around her, hers around me, holding hands, eyes fixated on each other. As tears poured down my cheeks, I asked her for forgiveness. Gwen replied, "I know that God has forgiven you and I forgive you also."

We talk about this moment often. Gwen recalls that this was the first time in years of marriage she saw love in my eyes.

Our second renewal was on our 25th wedding anniversary June 12' 1995. At a surprise party I asked Gwen if she would marry me…again. She yelled yes! I asked our pastor, who was in attendance, to re-marry us. Our daughter was the bride's maid and our sons were the best men. There was not a dry eye in the crowd. This was another red letter day and a NEW life together. Three years of sobriety were behind us and Gwen realized with certainty that her prayer had been really answered.

We continued to move. In the time since I became sober, we have moved from Roswell, Ga. to Miami, Fl., Singapore, Roswell, Ga. and Miami, Fl. and finally back to Alpharetta, Ga. In 2008, during a men's Souly Business retreat, I realized that Christ had forgiven me. What right did I have not to forgive myself? I finally forgave myself that weekend and took the burden I have carried for so many years off my shoulders and handed it to Jesus. I am free from the addiction of alcohol and I am "content" with Gwen and in our relationship together with Jesus Christ. My favorite Bible verse is Ecclesiastes 4:9-12:

"Two are better than one, because they have a good return for their work…

If one falls down, his friend can help him up…

But pity the man that falls and has n

one to help him up….

Also, if two lie down together, they will keep warm. But how can one keep warm alone?

Though one may be overpowered, two can

defend themselves

A cord of three strands is not quickly broken"

Ecclesiastes 4:9-12

I remember each day:

- Jesus does not promise that my life will be event free. What he does promise is that He will always be with me;

- Only Christ can live a Christian life not ME, I can not do it myself;
- I am at war every day and without Jesus I will fail;
- I Count my blessings and I try not to focus on the bad things;
- My relationship with Christ should not be moderately important;
- Verses I have hanging on my mirror:
    - John 15:11 “I have told you this so that my joy may be in you and that your joy may be complete.”
    - John 16:33 “I have told you these things, so that in me you may have peace. In this world you will have trouble. But take heart! I have overcome the world.”
    - Phillipians 4:11 “I have learned to be content whatever the circumstances.”

Am I ever going to get it right? *NO*. But**,** because of our Lord and Savior Jesus Christ, I have had second chances and I can keep trying. Because of HIS Grace, Love and Mercy, He is always at my side. Because of a praying wife, Jesus Christ saved me and answered her prayer for the restoration of the Godly man she knew she had married in 1970, twenty two years earlier. We will celebrate our 40th anniversary this June 12th.

Finally, 2 Corinthians 5:17 “Therefore, if anyone is in Christ, he is a new creation; the old has gone, the new has come!” Praise God!

Gary Grant:

I have been in the professional market place for 40 years. I worked ten years with NCR Corporation, fifteen years with VeriFone leading the US organization, Asia organization in Singapore and South American organization and I currently lead the Petroleum-C-Store division for the Royal Bank of Scotland. I am member of RUMC since 1988. I volunteer for Job Networking, Souly Business and True Identity ministries. I have been married 40 years and grandfather for six children under eight years old!

I can be reached at gary_g@bellsouth.net .

Dick's Story

My Life during the Great Depression, World War II and Now: A Brief Reflection

I was raised in Brooklyn, N.Y., along with thousands of other kids. This was in the 1920's when the Dodgers were the soul of Brooklyn. This was also a time of an in-pouring of immigrants. I met and knew a lot of families that did not speak or write English. The immigrants came with the hope of finding jobs in the "new land." Then the Great Depression hit. Virtually everyone was unemployed. The only safe industry was construction and there was much of that in the city: Empire State Building, Brooklyn Bridge, the subways and sewers. Any one lucky enough to get one of those jobs did not get a very big wage, just about enough to cover meal expenses for a family. Even though I was just a teenager, this made a huge impression on me.

I delivered newspapers: *The Chat, Brooklyn Union* and others. I even started my own business. I found a baby carriage, took the wheels off it and built a wagon. Next I went to the garment workers district along Broadway and picked up rags. I sold the rags and the old newspapers to the local junkies. They paid by the pound. I had two sources of income. I shared my income with the family to help take some of the load off my dad's back.

As did many who grew up in those times, I learned that when you make it, you save it. I also learned, never to buy "over your head" and to keep God in your life. I made a lot of friends in those days as I went about doing my jobs.

World War II began. Along with many others of my age, I enlisted to become part of those defending our nation. I signed up to join the U.S. Marines, five months and five days after the bombing of Pearl Harbor. I was sent to Parris Island, a unique cultural resort off the coast of South Carolina. For 14 weeks, we learned the fine art of punishing our bodies. I was given a test and sent to the Marine Air Force base at Cherry Point, N.C. From there I was assigned to school in Newport, R.I. to become an Electricians' Mate. From there I went back to Cherry Point. My next destination was the South Pacific. I arrived in time for the invasion of Ley-te in the Philippines. Then I went with the troops who liberated Luzon and Mindanao. I had a 30 day leave and came back in time to be involved in the preparations for the invasion of Japan. Fortunately, that never happened. During my leave, I married Viola, the girl of my dreams. We were married for 61 years when she died in September 2006.

I learned that when you make it, you save it. I also learned, never to buy "over your head" and to keep God in your life.

The war effort put a quick end to the Depression. But when I was discharged in September, 1945 and headed for home in Brooklyn, N.Y. I still worried about getting a job. I called my father-in-law from the base before I left and I asked if he could arrange for me to secure a job with the armored car companies. He did. While I worked, I went to school at night to learn television repair. When I finished my course, I started a TV repair business. So, now I was working two jobs. I didn't have much time to help others or serve others and I missed it.

During those years in Brooklyn, Viola and I had two girls, joined a church and bought a house. I realized I needed to make some changes because I missed being able to help others.

I had been active in church when I was a kid growing up. My aunt would come from Richmond Hills, in Queens, and take me to the nearby Lutheran church, every Sunday. This was quite a trip for her but she never complained. A kind gentleman named Mr. Apple gave me a dime every week when I came to church. That helped me form a church-going habit. As I grew older (about 10 or 11 years old), I joined a Lutheran church near home. I was confirmed there and I made some lifelong friends in that church. I always felt that God was on my right shoulder, guiding me, keeping me on the straight and narrow. I learned about volunteering there and began to feel the rewards of helping others. I had even been a Boy Scout as a lad. We delivered food baskets to the needy of the church and helped to serve church suppers.

In 1956, we sold our house in West Hempstead, N.Y. and we moved to Miami, Florida. Through a friend I found employment with National Airlines as a radio man. We purchased a house in Northwest Miami. I worked alternating shifts. Neither my wife and daughters, nor I, were very happy with that work routine. We did make friends at the church and we volunteered at various events. After two years and many challenges, we finally sold our house in Miami.

I called a friend on Long Island, in New York, who worked for Republic Airlines. I told him I needed a job. He told me to send my resume to him and he would see what he could do. A few days later he called to tell me he had set up an interview for me with the personnel department. I flew to Long Island, had my interview and was hired. After some time, my wife and our two daughters were able to join me.

We found a house in Huntington Station and moved in. We joined a nearby Lutheran church and very quickly became involved. My wife served on various food committees. I served on the Grounds Committee. About five of us served as a maintenance team for the church and as a result we saved the church considerable money and time.

Six years after going to work for Republic, a cut back in aircraft production led to lay-offs. I was among those who were laid off. Fortunately, within six weeks, I was back at work with the Grumman Corporation. I worked for Grumman for 21 years, until I retired in 1986.

During all those years, I volunteered at the church, where we made great friends and enjoyed all the activities. For the most part, my life experiences taught me not to be afraid of anything when working on God's behalf.

After I retired, Viola and I moved to Florida and bought a home. We lived there for 13 years. In 2000, because of my wife's failing health and heart surgery, we moved to Georgia at the request of our daughter and her husband. They introduced us to the people at their church, Roswell United Methodist Church. We liked the members and the pastors. We joined the Seekers Sunday School Class and have been there ever since.

When my beloved Vi passed away in 2006, I had a lot of time on my hands so I served on dinner committees at the church, became President of the Seekers Class, involved myself in the Senior Center and volunteered with Job Networking.

I am in my 80's and have been out of the workforce for a long time. But I still remember the Depression and I remember people being out of work and families struggling. I can help make a difference in the lives of families that deal with unemployment today. I help in any way I can. I work where I am most needed each time we meet. I enjoy working first hand with God's people. I like being part of a great volunteer effort. When each meeting ends, I walk away feeling blessed.

Richard (Dick) Fritz:

I came into this world and was named Richard A Fritz. My father was my hero and my aunts were my guiding angels. My daughter is the author of this book. I worked in the aircraft industry most of my working career, attended many electronic courses and then went to the company from which I eventually retired. But in all those years my greatest pleasure was volunteering for the church. It was and is GOD's work.

Mike Long

Senior Pastor, Roswell United Methodist Church

A Unique Look from the Senior Pastor

He called a few days after Christmas and asked if we could meet. When I asked him how he knew to call me, he said, "I have been to Job Networking several times. Your church has been so helpful; I just need to talk to somebody, so I thought I would call you."

He wanted to talk about a relationship with his girlfriend and his willingness to renew his relationship with the Lord. Throughout the conversation, he kept thanking our church for the volunteers who helped him when he was in his "career transition." He had recently gone through another job search with renewed confidence because of what he had learned in our Job Networking Ministry.

But today he just needed to talk to a minister, to think through some relationship issues, and to reconnect with the Lord. Because our church had ministered to him in the past, he knew he could call on us again.

Through Job Networking, our caring volunteers love on hurting people, offer new ideas for Job Seekers, and provide encouragement in challenging times. We meet people where they are and offer to walk with them in their career transitions.

From this pastor's perspective, I observe passionate disciples living and sharing their faith. I see lay people being the church and becoming the compassionate hands of Christ. I watch caring volunteers experience the joy of being in ministry and making a profound difference in the lives of others.

My heart is warmed as these passionate disciples open their hearts to their neighbors. So when I got a call from this person that I did not know, we met and talked and prayed. We got together because the Job Networking volunteers have reminded me to love my neighbor.

Dr. Michael H. Long:

Mike attended Candler School of Theology and was ordained an elder in 1982. In 1992, he received his Doctorate of Ministry from McCormick Theology Seminary. Since 2001, Mike has served as the Senior Minister of Roswell United Methodist Church.

ABOUT THE AUTHOR

Katherine Simons

I am a Volunteer Leader at the RUMC Job Networking Ministry and a member of RUMC since 1982. I have prior work experience as an owner of a healthcare staffing company, which I sold 3 years ago and in which I am still participating. I now use my time to volunteer for this ministry, HomeStretch, the North Fulton Chamber of Commerce, and I serve on the Board of Directors for Atlanta Business Bank. My two married daughters grew up in this church and still live near us. They added two "sons" to our family. My husband and my dad are both active in this ministry as many of our closest friends and Sunday school class members. The best part is I am married 42 years and the grandmother for 7 children,

I can be reached at WWW.lovingyourneighbor.com .